Dyslexia:

Assessing the need for Access Arrangements during Examinations

A Practical Guide

Fourth Edition

Edited by

Anwen Jones

Additional copies of this book may be ordered from
Patoss Ltd
PO Box 10
Evesham
Worcestershire
WR11 1ZW

Telephone: 01386 712650
Fax: 01386 712716

Order forms are also available from our website: www.patoss-dyslexia.org

Published by
Patoss

The Professional Association of Teachers of Students
with Specific Learning Difficulties Ltd
P O Box 10, Evesham, Worcestershire, WR11 6ZW
Tel: 01386 712650

e-mail: *patoss@sworcs.ac.uk*
website: *www.patoss-dyslexia.org*

with thanks to Gill Backhouse

In furthering good practice we are very pleased to publish this fourth edition of 'A Practical Guide'. It has been written to support the Joint Council's regulations and provide a 'how to' guide in approaching the entire area of exam access arrangements for SpLD students in schools and colleges. It is an essential resource for anyone involved in the process and replaces all previous editions.

Patoss, The Professional Association of Teachers of Students with Specific Learning Difficulties, was formed in 1987 and is now an international association of teachers and other professionals working in the field of specific learning difficulties with individuals across the educational spectrum from primary to adult. Our association serves to:

- establish and maintain the professional status of those qualified to teach and assess students with specific learning difficulties
- give a professional corporate response to the Government departments on matters affecting SpLD students
- promote the continued provision and development of appropriate specialist qualifications in the teaching of students with SpLD
- promote links with teachers working with SpLD students in all sectors of education and with other professionals involved in the field of SpLD and promote fuller understanding and recognition of SpLD
- enable members to update and extend their knowledge and skills and to exchange ideas through an annual association conference, bulletins and local groups.

Membership is open to teachers with approved qualifications in SpLD, students working towards an SpLD qualification, other professionally qualified individuals, and all schools, colleges or organisations with a professional interest in SpLD. Among the services we provide are:

- a member's e-mail helpline to assist with queries relating to SpLD assessment and practice
- professional indemnity insurance scheme for appropriately qualified members
- facilities for CRB checks
- SpLD Assessment Practising Certificates and Teaching Practising Certificates
- Tutor / Assessor Index
- a range of other publications including a resources guide, bulletins and newsletters
- a website with useful information for the public and members
- SpLD continuing professional development events

We are delighted to once again work with the JCQ and look forward to continuing to do so in the future.

Lynn Greenwold

Chief Executive

The Joint Council for Qualifications (JCQ) was formed in January 2004 and replaced the JCGQ. The JCQ consists of AQA, City & Guilds, CCEA, Edexcel, OCR, SQA, and WJEC, the seven largest providers of qualifications in the UK, offering GCSE, GCE, Entry Level, Basic, Functional and Key Skills, Diploma, Vocational and Occupational qualifications.

The JCQ was formed to enable the member awarding bodies to act together to provide, wherever possible, common administrative arrangements for the schools, colleges and other providers that offer their qualifications. In this respect the small team at the JCQ acts as an administrative hub for the joint and collaborative work of the members.

All joint regulations, guidance, forms, other administrative documents, systems and procedures are produced through collaborative working and are introduced and used with the agreement of the members. The JCQ works with the awarding bodies to develop and agree the regulations and arrangements. The JCQ badge is used to denote where the awarding bodies have acted together.

The JCQ and the awarding bodies have worked together for many years to produce and update regulations and guidance for access arrangements for examinations in general qualifications (GCSE, GCE, Entry Level, Basic, Functional and Key Skills). Each year the regulations and guidance are reviewed and developed in the light of best practice.

In recent years the JCQ regulations have been updated to take account of the Disability Discrimination Act (DDA) 1995, the introduction of an online system to process applications (Access arrangements online) and will be updated to reflect the introduction of the Equality Act 2010.

We are pleased to continue to work in association with Patoss to produce further guidance for the teachers and staff who produce the reports needed to support applications for access arrangements for students taking general qualifications. This booklet provides invaluable information for teachers and will help to ensure that these candidates are appropriately supported and receive the access arrangements to which they are entitled, thereby maintaining fairness across the examinations system.

Dr. Jim Sinclair
Director

Table of Contents

Acknowledgements

Gill Backhouse was the author of the first three editions of this Patoss Guide and it is to her that this fourth edition is dedicated. Gill has inspired, supported, guided and informed many education professionals through her work as a psychologist and teacher-trainer; her overall contribution to the understanding and practice of support for individuals with SpLDs should not be understated. Gill continues to work and write in the SpLD field and a new publication with guidance for SENCOs is in press. However, in regard to this Guide she has generously released all intellectual property rights to Patoss.

Contributors to the fourth edition

Anwen Jones is the current Programme Director at Patoss. She leads professional training and provides assessment guidance to Specialist Teachers. Formerly a learning support co-ordinator with responsibility for access arrangements, she continues to assess and teach students with SpLD.

Nick Lait has provided an updated introduction to the JCQ regulations (Chapter 2) and has contributed throughout this Guide to the interpretation of the regulations. Nick is the Examinations and Committee Manager at the JCQ, where his responsibilities encompass production of the JCQ access arrangement regulations, provision of Centre support through training events and advice and guidance in regard to access arrangements.

Caroline Read has again contributed a chapter providing step-by-step guidance to school SENCOs through the access arrangement year (Chapter 7). Caroline is a Specialist Teacher based in a secondary school and a consultant, course tutor and writer for Communicate-ed.

Lynn Greenwold is Patoss Chief Executive, current Chair of the Dyslexia-SpLD Trust and the SpLD Assessment Standards Committee. She has provided a comprehensive overview of this Guide.

We are also particularly indebted to **Jen McDermott** and **Debby Ardley**, who undertook the test reviews for this Guide, and also to Louise Green. A number of other people have also made valued contributions to individual chapters or the proof-reading process and sincere thanks go to them: Gill Backhouse, Jonathan Bishop, Judy Capener, Cate Evans, Marie Garner, David Grant, Sylvia Moody and Jane Rickey.

Finally, mention must be made of the ongoing support provided by the administrative team at Patoss without whom this publication simply would not be in your hands: Sue Lashley, Alison Jeanes and Mandy Williams.

Introduction

"Much has changed" was the opening sentiment in the last edition of this Guide, published in 2007, and the same can be said again in 2011.

- The landscape, at least the paperwork landscape, has changed dramatically with the introduction of Access Arrangements Online, the system to provide instant decisions on arrangements for GCSE and GCE 'A' level examinations.

- The Equality Act 2010 has brought a new legislative framework, although the underlying principles are substantially unchanged.

- The recent Rose Review (2009) - *Identifying and Teaching Children and Young People with Dyslexia and Literacy Difficulties* - has raised awareness of the needs for effective assessment and support for individuals with SpLD, and development continues following the *SpLD / DfES Working Party Report 2005* to support best practice in assessment.

- The JCQ regulations have continued to be revised and updated, with more arrangement decisions delegated to Centres; this trend will continue in 2011/12.

However, the principles guiding access arrangements remain unchanged. They seek to support candidates to show their knowledge and skills without compromising the qualifications they subsequently gain. These access arrangements are a hugely beneficial part of support for students with SpLDs, but only a part. Learning support to develop independent skills must still be the primary goal of all concerned. This can be a challenge, especially in a period of change and immense pressure on resources, but I hope this Guide supports continued best practice and promotes an equitable system for all.

As with previous editions, the convention of referring to all teachers as though they were female and all candidates as though they were male has been followed. Also, knowledge of the most common acronyms in our field is assumed and they are used without further expansion, but a list is provided at the end of the text.

I extend my sincere personal thanks to all those who have contributed to this publication.

Anwen Jones

Patoss

April 2011

1. The JCQ Regulations & Guidance - Essential Reading

Each autumn the Joint Council for Qualifications (JCQ) publishes a revised document setting out its regulations and guidance for the forthcoming academic year: *Access Arrangements, Reasonable Adjustments and Special Consideration – General and Vocational Qualifications*. This concerns examinations leading to awards from JCQ members – AQA, Edexcel, CCEA, City & Guilds, OCR and WJEC. This publication – also known as "the pink book" - is sent to all Centres at the beginning of the autumn term and can also be downloaded from the JCQ website (www.jcq.org.uk).

All personnel involved with candidates who have special assessment needs must have their own copy of the **current** regulations. The Patoss Guide supports, but does not replace, the JCQ publication which is the primary reference and must be carefully read and followed. This edition of the Guide has been written in accordance with the regulations for 1 September 2010 – 31 August 2011. No responsibility is taken by Patoss, the Editor, or the contributing authors for any misunderstandings or failure to comply with the JCQ regulations during this, or subsequent years.

The Patoss Guide is no substitute for reading the full JCQ document each year.

Of particular note are the sections placed right at the beginning of the JCQ regulations: *Deadlines for Submitting Applications for Access Arrangements and Modified Papers Online for GCSE and GCE Qualifications* and **Changes for the Academic Year** as these are particularly significant for Centres.

Access arrangements are available to candidates with physical disabilities, sensory impairments and **learning difficulties**. This Guide focuses on assessing and meeting the needs of the latter group. This process often requires an assessment report prepared by an appropriately qualified Specialist Teacher or Psychologist. Their role is to assist Centres by providing evidence of learning difficulties, not to make a decision themselves – an important point for independent practitioners approached directly by candidates or their parents.

All applications for GCSE / GCE candidates are now managed through the **Access Arrangements Online** (AAO) system. For other qualifications, a paper-based system remains in place. Regardless of the application method, equivalent evidence standards apply and Centres must maintain thorough records of support given to candidates; the JCQ section headed **Synopsis of Access Arrangements and Evidence Requirements** shows what is needed for each type of arrangement. A number of arrangements no longer require formal evidence, although it is expected they will still reflect the candidate's normal way of working.

Regardless of changes to administration or adjustments to regulations, the over-arching principle to support equality of access to assessment remains the same. Discussions of the roles of all involved in achieving this goal – the **Head of Centre, Exams Officer, SENCO, ALS Manager, Subject and Specialist Teachers** – are to be found later in this Guide.

2. Understanding & Implementing the JCQ Regulations

by Nick Lait

Introduction

Previous editions of this Patoss Guide have been greatly appreciated by both teaching staff and the JCQ, who have found it an invaluable resource in giving advice to those assessing candidates for access arrangements. Those working within the JCQ office or an Awarding Body (AB) are laymen and women in this field, yet are often the first port of call for Teachers and Psychologists faced with difficulties.

Patoss and the JCQ have been consulting with each other with the aim of strengthening the working relationship between Centres and the JCQ so access arrangements can meet the needs of candidates while maintaining the validity of qualifications. It is the JCQ's key aim that the qualifications of a candidate with access arrangements should be seen to have the same credibility as those of any other candidate. In order to do that, we have to make sure that all candidates meet the same requirements in examinations and are assessed in the same way.

The move towards greater inclusion has seen more access arrangements being processed by Centres. The Disability Discrimination Act (DDA) applied to General Qualifications in September 2007 and resulted in a number of changes to the JCQ regulations, making arrangements more equitable across all types of disability. The Equality Act (2010) has now superseded the DDA, and the JCQ will be working to update their regulations in light of the new Act.

In September 2008 the process of applying for access arrangements was revamped, being modernised for the 21st century. Access Arrangements Online (AAO) was introduced allowing applications to be processed online, with a single, instant decision. This online system has significantly reduced paperwork and bureaucracy for Centres. In over 93% of cases, AAO is handling applications, with evidence kept on file within the Centre for inspection purposes. Additionally, since September 2009, the JCQ has removed 11 access arrangements from AAO, and will remove a further 2 in September 2011, allowing Centres to simply make the decision as to whether the candidate needs the arrangement(s).

To inform all decisions Teachers must read the JCQ regulations carefully each year. So often people rely on or misinterpret what someone else has told them and then find themselves in difficulties when 'an Inspector calls'! Please do not leave yourself without adequate evidence that the candidate is eligible for the arrangement, especially those processed online or Centre-delegated which you have subsequently allowed.

We hope that you will use this book alongside your copy of the JCQ regulations as well as AAO. They complement one another and need to be used together. As the JCQ regulations change slightly every year you must keep constantly up to date with changes in order to give the best service to your candidates.

Finding your way

One of the problems when beginning any discussion about access arrangements is that we are entering into a world of jargon and often misunderstanding. Most people think that they understand the issues until they try to have a conversation, whether this is between the parents and the Examinations Officer, between the Examinations Officer and the Specialist Teacher, between the Subject Teacher and the Specialist Teacher or between the Examinations Officer and the JCQ office or an AB.

Let us begin with a 'Who's Who' of people involved.

The Candidate	This is the person taking the examination. The term refers to male and female, young and old and is therefore the preferred term used in this context.
The Parent/Carer/Guardian	This is the person with personal responsibility for the candidate. The role of this person will be explained below.
The Centre	This is the school or college where the examination is to take place and normally is the place where the course has been taught.
The Examinations Officer	This is the administrator in the Centre who has responsibility for the examinations. This person makes the entries, may process access arrangements and submit requests for modified papers.
The SENCO	This is the Special Educational Needs co-ordinator who co-ordinates the education of pupils with disabilities and learning difficulties. He/she may also process access arrangements and submit requests for modified papers.
The Specialist Teacher	This is the teacher who carries out the diagnostic assessment of needs. The Specialist Teacher and the SENCO may be the same person if the SENCO is appropriately qualified to carry out diagnostic testing and has been approved by their Head of Centre.
The Subject Teacher	This is the person who teaches the candidate the individual subject(s) and who needs to talk to the Examinations Officer about which examinations are to be entered in each series. The Subject Teacher may need to seek or give advice about the reasonableness of an adjustment or arrangement in the context of the assessment objectives being tested in the qualification.
The Awarding Body (AB)	This used to be called an Examinations Board. It is the organisation responsible for producing the examination papers, grading the candidates' work and issuing the results.

The Joint Council for Qualifications (JCQ)	The ABs work together through the JCQ which has its own Director and staff. The JCQ publishes a common set of rules to make sure access arrangements are appropriate and consistent.
The Regulators	Each country in the UK has regulators who are responsible for ensuring that ABs carry out their work according to an agreed procedure, commonly known as the Code of Practice.

What does the terminology mean?

Entries	These are technically the orders for the question papers and other materials. The Examinations Officer submits them by fixed deadlines. It is very important to meet the deadlines if the question papers are to arrive in time. Entries are also made for controlled assessments/coursework so that marks can be submitted.
Assessment	This word includes written examinations, and the coursework which are two different types of assessment. It also includes practical tests, performing tests and speaking tests.
Assessment Objectives	These are the knowledge, understanding and skills being tested in the assessment. They might include how much geography the candidate knows but also how well the candidate can analyse a set of geographical data. They might also include how well the candidate can speak French, model clay, or build a working machine.
Diagnostic Assessment	The investigation undertaken by a qualified assessor, either a Specialist Teacher or Psychologist, of the candidate's learning difficulties.
Access Arrangements	These are arrangements made before the examination, such as extra time or allowing a candidate to use a scribe. They are based on need but must also meet the requirements of the assessment. The candidate gains marks for skills he can carry out, so the arrangement must not allow anyone else to do something which will gain marks for the candidate.
Reasonable Adjustments	Reasonable adjustments are required by law for candidates who are disabled under the terms of the Equality Act 2010. There is no duty to make a reasonable adjustment in respect of a competence standard.
Referral	If AAO rejects an application you may refer the case online to the awarding body, although a careful review of the regulations is essential beforehand.
Regulations	Every year the JCQ publishes a booklet of regulations relating to access arrangements and special consideration. They are sent to Centres but are also available on the JCQ website www.jcq.org.uk

Special Consideration	This is a small adjustment to the marks given when the candidate knows the work but is too ill at the time of the assessment to show what he or she can do. It cannot compensate for not being able to carry out the tasks being tested or missing large sections of the course.
Examination Series	These are the months when examinations are timetabled and controlled assessment/coursework marks have to be submitted.
Results	The results are based on the marking of each part of the assessment. All candidates have to be measured according to the same mark scheme, so that their results have the same value. Those with access arrangements or special consideration receive valid results as long as all the regulations have been followed.
Appeals	If the Centre is not satisfied with the grading or the special consideration awarded, the Examinations Officer may ask the Awarding Body for further explanation. The Head of Centre may then wish to take the matter to the Appeals Committee of the Awarding Body involved. The Appeals Committees are made up of independent people who are not employed by the Awarding Body. They cannot change the regulations but they can ensure that the decision has been made according to the rules and the agreed procedures, and is fair and consistent. Only the Head of Centre can make an appeal to these Committees.
Malpractice	If the Awarding Body is not satisfied that the assessment has been carried out according to the regulations and feels that access arrangements have given the candidate an unfair advantage, the Head of Centre may be asked to carry out an investigation. The outcome can vary from a warning to removal of the Centre's registration.

What happens in the course of the year?

September	Course begins. Examinations Officer orders enlarged or modified papers. Take special note of those taking examinations in November and/or January. Awarding Body staff are busy taking enquiries about results from previous June and getting papers ready for January.
October	Examinations Officer processes applications online for access arrangements for those taking examinations in November and January. Specialist Teachers are busy assessing candidates for June.
November	Some GCSE examinations take place, mainly Maths and Science. Some AB and JCQ staff now take summer holidays!
December	Christmas! Staff are all still busy but do take a break!
January	More examinations take place. Examinations Officer orders any additional modified papers for those taking examinations in June. Examinations Officer processes emergency access arrangements and submits applications for special consideration for those who are ill in January – watch out for winter epidemics or broken arms from skiing trips!
February	Examinations Officer makes GCSE entries and processes applications online for access arrangements in June.
March	More examinations. More entries for GCE AS and A2 units and GCSE re-sit entries following receipt of January results.
April	Controlled assessments/coursework are being completed. Don't lose it or wrap it in bin bags! Keep marks separately from the work.
May	Controlled assessments/coursework marks are sent in. First summer examinations start. Examinations Officer processes emergency access arrangements online using AAO. Special consideration applications submitted to awarding bodies.
June	Examinations continue. SENCO, Examinations Officer and AB staff are run off their feet.
July	Centre staff collapse and go on holiday. Awarding Body staff are busy grading, checking and reviewing marking.
August	Checking is finished and results are issued. Enquiries start again.

The problem is that these processes merge with one another and before one is finished, the next one has begun.

This schedule applies substantially to GCSE and GCE examinations. Yet, schools and colleges are now involved in delivering many other types and formats of qualifications – all with their own processes and schedules – so all involved must be familiar with the particular needs of their Centre.

What can each person do to make sure everything is in place on time?

The Parent / Carer / Guardian should make sure that any paperwork required is available on time and is up to date. This might be a medical report for a candidate with long–term illness or it might be a report prepared by a qualified Psychologist or a Specialist Teacher. There are rules about how old a report can be if it is to be accepted. Much valuable time is wasted if parents try to by-pass the regulations and engage in a personal battle with the JCQ or an AB. The way to achieve the best possible outcome for the candidate is to make sure everyone knows how to proceed in an organised and calm fashion so that every application is dealt with in order and in time for the examinations. The JCQ and the ABs will not deal directly with parents.

The Candidate should make sure that his or her needs are known to the Centre and that the Examinations Officer has everything needed to process appropriate access arrangements on time. Adult candidates should check that they are seen by a specialist at the right time.

The Examinations Officer, the Subject Teacher and the SENCO must talk to one another. They need to be clear about whether the subject will have assessments or examinations in any of the early series, in November, January or March. They need to be clear about which code numbers to use in order to request modified papers. They need to be clear about what the needs of a particular candidate are, what arrangements have been made during the course, what skills are being tested in each subject and which arrangements are appropriate to request. If the candidates need to be assessed, the SENCO must make appointments with Specialist Teachers or Psychologists in good time, preferably at the beginning of the course. The Examinations Officer must then make sure that any arrangements are processed in time using AAO and that those which have been agreed are put in place in accordance with the rules. Where required, the Examinations Officer must ensure that appropriate evidence is on file to substantiate the arrangement(s) for when an "Inspector calls".

The AB will process requests for modified papers and deal with the small number of on-line referrals. They will liaise with the Examinations Officer or Head of Centre. It is not the JCQ's or an AB's role to tell Specialist Teachers how to assess candidates. Advice relating to diagnostic assessments should come from the provider of the specialist qualification.

Remember, the candidate who gets the best deal is the one whose parents and teachers work together as a team, in an organised and courteous manner and whose business with the Awarding Body is conducted in a professional and timely way.

Three Cautionary Tales

1.   Mr. Wright is a new Examinations Officer and knows that he is facing a tough year. He opens his copy of the new regulations in September and reads it from cover to cover. He knows all his deadlines and prepares to process the reports which have been prepared earlier by his very reliable Specialist Teacher. Miss Calculate, the Mathematics teacher, has in her class a candidate with a severe visual impairment. She tells the Examinations Officer in good time that he will want an A4 18 point bold modified enlarged paper for the March series and gives him the code number for the Foundation Tier. Mr. Wright orders the correct paper and the AB arranges for the paper to be modified and printed. On the day of the examination, the candidate opens the paper but it is the wrong one. The Mathematics teacher had changed her mind about the paper, preparing the candidate for the Higher Tier but forgot to tell the Examinations Officer!!

2.   Ms. Phile is a well-organised SENCO. At the start of every September, she sends a list around to collect information about which of her special needs pupils are likely to be entering for examinations in the current year. She then arranges for them to be tested by a Specialist Teacher or Psychologist according to the number of appointments she can make with each. She gives all the parents the dates and times of the appointments. They go to be tested and she carefully files all the reports. She then notices that one is missing and telephones Mr. Sloth to ask whether he took his son to be assessed for a reader and extra time of up to 25%. Mr. Sloth says he missed the appointment but he had not bothered to tell her this and time is running out. She quickly telephones round to see if she can make another appointment. Everyone is booked up. The only date she can get is in May. Mr. Sloth takes his son to the Specialist on 12th May but his first examination is on 15th May. The report does not get to the Centre in time to be processed online for the candidate's first exam, so his son has to manage without a reader and extra time of up to 25% for his exam on 15th May.

3.   Miss Place is an over-worked and stressed Examinations Officer. She is contacted by Mrs. Calling-Daily about her daughter who needs a scribe. Miss Place remembers to tell her what is required and Mrs. Calling-Daily takes her daughter to be assessed and gives the report in good time to Miss Place. She puts it on her desk. The next day, a member of the school office staff brings in the post and puts it on top of the report. It disappears, filed with other documents. Miss Place forgets that she has not processed the report for the access arrangements. All through March and April, Mrs. Calling-Daily telephones the school but the report cannot be found and the writer of the report has now retired and cannot be contacted. Mrs. Calling-Daily did not keep a copy. She telephones the JCQ but they have not heard about her daughter. Then she telephones her MP and the DfE and the local press. Miss Place goes on sick leave. The candidate takes her examination but she cannot have a scribe because an application was not processed online and there is no evidence to support one.

Why do the Regulations Change?

There are several reasons why regulations have changed over the years. Some are simply for practical reasons, some have their roots in changes of thinking resulting from research undertaken by the regulators, some have arisen through the introduction of disability legislation and others as a consequence of AAO.

Over the years, Centres have sought clarification about how to interpret the regulations so amendments are made every year to spell out some of the sections which have prompted enquiries.

Disability Awareness

As time has passed, different disability groups have become more aware of the possibility of taking examinations and attempts have been made to accommodate their needs as far as possible without changing the quality of the assessment and the qualification those candidates will obtain.

The Equality Act 2010

The JCQ regulations will be amended in order to meet the requirements of the Equality Act 2010, which will apply to general qualifications.

In order to make provision as consistent and fair as possible across the different disability groups, ABs are working towards the modification of carrier language in question papers so that the standard paper should be suitable for candidates with comprehension difficulties, irrespective of the reason for the impairment. As papers are prepared so far in advance of the examination series, this has to be a phased approach but some papers have already been modified in this way. Technical language and abstract concepts will not be removed as these will be part of the assessment objectives being tested but the aim is to remove unnecessary barriers to comprehension by removing complicated sentence structures when they are not essential to the question itself.

Technological developments continue to be discussed with regard to adapting modified papers to be read on screen, and several small-scale pilots took place in 2008 and 2009. However, progress is slow and funding is needed to pursue such a strategy on a much wider scale.

Why was your Request Rejected?

1. Assessment Objectives

The major issue for parents and Specialist Teachers is the question, "Why was my application rejected?" The JCQ regulations contain a short chapter on the assessment objectives. The major reason for refusing a request is that the candidate has to demonstrate that particular skill in order to gain the qualification. You could not issue a driving licence to a candidate who could not see. Similarly, you cannot give a music qualification to a candidate who cannot play the instrument required by the specification, or a sports qualification to a candidate who cannot take part in any of the specified sports. If the examination is testing reading, the candidate must be able to read. If it is testing speaking, the candidate must be able to speak. Candidates can, however, attempt those parts of the assessment which they can manage and gain marks accordingly.

2. Eligibility

Another reason for refusing the request is that the candidate can manage to read or write independently and should be doing so. The regulations have always tried to define those candidates who are most in need of assistance, so that the reading and writing assistance is reserved for those with a substantial impairment. It should be remembered that qualifications are the gateway to employment or further/higher education. The qualification must give a realistic picture to the employer of what he might expect the candidate to be able to do.

Some Centres seem to be unaware of the fact that since 1998 candidates with moderate learning difficulties have also been included for arrangements in the JCQ regulations.

Candidates with less severe impairments may be eligible to have arrangements which have a lesser effect on the assessment. A candidate might not be eligible to use a scribe but might be able to use a word processor, for instance, or have extra time of up to 25%.

How do you know which arrangement is appropriate?

The JCQ regulations contain a chapter about each of the access arrangements you can apply for and also tell you that some arrangements are not available in some subjects. Other sections of this Guide will advise you how to go about deciding who needs extra help, which tests to use and how to interpret the results of these tests. You end up with a list of people whose needs are all very different. **Let us begin with the most severely affected.**

Severe Writing Difficulties

There is no difficulty in dealing with a candidate who cannot write at all, either because of a physical or visual difficulty or because the candidate's learning difficulty is so severe that the tests come out with well below average scores. For example:

- spelling is so poor that the reader cannot understand what the candidate is trying to convey.

- writing is so badly formed that the words cannot be read and he is not confident using a word processor.

- the effort is such that the candidate composes a few lines of immature prose in the time it would take the same candidate to dictate a page and a half of interesting information.

This candidate may need a scribe. (It is unlikely that a candidate with such problems would be entering for Modern Foreign Languages but if so, the scribe would not be allowed in the writing papers unless the candidate could spell out every letter.)

Then there is a candidate with similar problems but who *is* proficient in using a word processor and uses it as part of his normal daily work. The appropriate arrangement in this case is not to ask for a scribe but to allow him to use a word processor with the spell check enabled. This is an independent form of written communication and far more preferable to having to rely on a third party if the candidate doesn't need to. There are rules relating to how word processors are set up to ensure that they do not interfere with the assessment.

Alternatively, the Centre may decide that for a candidate whose writing is very messy a transcript would be preferable. The teachers can read his writing but it is not very easy for a stranger to read it. This candidate needs a transcript written after the examination.

The choice between these three writing arrangements is therefore one relating to the current needs of the candidate, what the candidate is used to doing and what is most appropriate for the examination concerned. It is preferable to have more candidates using a word processor than a scribe as this better prepares them for Further Education, Higher Education and the world of employment. Word processing helps with their organisation of material, presentation, and their frequent omissions. In some cases it eases their inhibition about writing by hand or dictating to another person.

The use of a 'human' scribe should always be an arrangement of the last resort - you might first consider use of a word processor, voice-recognition software or a transcript. These arrangements allow the AB to receive a script which is the candidate's own work; a typed script is presented, by means of a word processor, or a written script accompanied by a transcript.

The candidate might therefore use technology in extended writing papers such as English, English Literature, and History because it reflects his normal way of working in those subjects. In subjects such as Maths and Science, where writing is more limited, a transcript is used since his teachers can read his writing.

Severe Reading Difficulties

The same guiding principles as noted above apply to reading difficulties: current need, current way of working and the demands of the assessment. You might ask for example:

- Does the candidate read independently and accurately?

- Does he read so slowly that the examination will be over before he has read the first page?

- Is the examination testing reading? GCSE English units now have sections testing reading and sections testing writing. You need to check with the English teacher, as reading assistance will be permitted in the writing section only.

- Do you have to provide reading assistance on a daily basis? If reading assistance in examinations is more occasional would the candidate benefit from a modified language paper? Or access to a reader in a small group?

There is a range of reading support options available and careful selection of the most appropriate arrangement for the individual must be the priority.

Borderline Cases

The biggest difficulty arises at the other end of the spectrum, when the candidate seems to have problems which have not previously been identified, so no history of provision exists, or where the impact is less immediately obvious. These are the borderline cases where the candidate might be performing at an age appropriate level but seems to be achieving more when working without time pressures or when contributing orally to discussion rather than handing in written work. If in doubt, you can actively monitor if the candidate appears to need extra time, or another arrangement as appropriate, in class tests and mock exams and then, if necessary, arrange for a diagnostic assessment by a Specialist Teacher or Psychologist. These cases are discussed further in Chapters 3 and 8 in particular.

When appropriate arrangements have been given to an eligible candidate, how will the script be marked?

The scripts of candidates with access arrangements are marked according to the same marking criteria as any other script. The assessment of written communication skill is carried out slightly differently from one subject to another, as the emphasis on language is different from subject to subject. Examiners will give credit for what the candidate can do.

Examples
(Please note, these examples are illustrations only and are not binding on any AB's Examining Teams)

a) A candidate uses a scribe in GCSE Science. A question includes the information that one mark is to be credited for spelling, punctuation and grammar. The Principal Examiner explains to the examining team that the mark is to be deducted if more than one error is made in either spelling, punctuation or grammar per sentence. The candidate using the scribe is using correct grammar and has dictated the punctuation but his spelling was that of the scribe and not his own. He cannot be given the mark, as this would be unfair to any candidate who had made several spelling errors.

b) Another candidate taking the same subject and also using a scribe dictates the spelling in each of the answers where written communication is being assessed and this has been noted on the JCQ Cover Sheet accompanying his script. He can be credited with the mark because he has made only one error. (Some candidates are not able to dictate spelling because they have so much difficulty dictating whole words and are very slow completing a sentence. They cannot receive the mark.)

c) A candidate uses a scribe in GCE History. The marking criteria are arranged in bands with a description of what has to be achieved to attain the mark for that band. A best-fit approach is taken. That means that the candidate is placed in the band which best describes the standard of the answer. The candidate is able to fulfill most of the criteria described in a particular band of marks and uses vocabulary well to express his arguments. However, he is not producing his own spelling. The highest band in the mark scheme requires the writing to show accuracy (but not perfection) in grammar, punctuation and spelling. The candidate is using grammar correctly but has not dictated any punctuation and has not produced the spelling. A decision has to be made as to whether he should be placed lower in the same band. This would be the same decision that would be made about any other candidate whose spelling was very weak but who had given a very good answer.

How can you appeal?

Only the Head of Centre can make appeals. For example, a Centre makes an application using AAO which is rejected. The Centre considers making an online referral to the AB. However, firstly the Centre must check the regulations, the subject specification and the results given in the specialist assessment report. If the candidate does not meet the published criteria for the arrangement, then there is little point in pursuing a referral. If a referral is also rejected, any subsequent appeal may be made by following the formal appeals procedure available for download from the JCQ website.

When can you apply for special consideration?

The JCQ regulations contain a chapter about who is eligible for special consideration and how it is applied. You will need to read it if you have any candidates who are ill, injured or bereaved at the time of the examinations, as they may be eligible for special consideration.

Special consideration is not an alternative for those who have a permanent disability or difficulty. Those candidates should have had an access arrangement application made for them well in advance of the examination, so they can take the examination. There can be no compensation for the fact that some candidates with disabilities may not be able to do some of the questions or perform some of the tasks. The examination is measuring what candidates know and can do, not what they might have achieved if the disability had not existed. It is therefore not appropriate to try to enhance marks for a skill which cannot be performed by the candidate.

If the candidate has been permitted an arrangement which the Centre failed to put in place, the Examinations Officer can apply for special consideration. It is a very small adjustment to the marks but it may help the candidate whose overall mark has fallen just below the next grade boundary. It is not an alternative to having the candidates assessed for access arrangements, as special consideration is given only when all of the correct procedures have been followed and it is clear that the candidate was eligible for the arrangement at the time of the examination. Centres should therefore take great care they put in place all approved arrangements not only because the consequences for candidates can be serious but so might the consequences of any complaint!

3. Principles Underlying Access Arrangements

The underlying rationale for access arrangements is very clear. They exist to provide reasonable adjustments to allow equality of access to assessment in education. They aim simply to allow candidates the opportunity "**to show what they know or can do without changing the demands of the assessment**"[1]. They must not confer any unfair advantage for those who receive them, and credit cannot be given for skills that cannot be demonstrated. All involved in the process should ensure that the principles of access arrangements are upheld in order that the integrity and credibility of qualifications and arrangements is maintained.

Given this principle, access arrangements can be awarded to those with a special educational need (SEN), a disability or a learning difficulty. The potential effects of such disabilities during examinations, as well as every day study, vary in nature and degree. It is the responsibility of the Centre to monitor students' difficulties and make appropriate arrangements for examinations.

When applying for access arrangements there are two main issues to be considered in relation to each candidate:

1. Has the candidate been entered for examinations which are at the right level, given his *level of general ability & attainments in each particular subject*?

2. What are the implications and degree of the candidate's *current difficulties* during examinations with *reading* the questions and *responding in writing*? How does he normally cope with reading and writing? Access arrangements should reflect his usual method of working (i.e. slowly / with a reader or scribe / using a word processor etc.)

Examinations are **qualifications** and are not designed to reflect a candidate's potential, rather the knowledge and skills he has demonstrated in the modules, coursework and final examination. His marks show the degree to which his work has met the published assessment objectives. This will depend on a variety of factors – how well he has been taught, how much effective work he has put in over the course and his examination technique; as well as his general underlying ability and his aptitude for each particular subject. Minor inaccuracies in spelling are unlikely to affect his final results significantly. There is a wide variation in the accuracy and speed of reading and writing skills across the population – as with every other human characteristic – and such normal variance is not cause for access arrangements.

The clear message from the JCQ is that the only learning difficulties meriting significant adjustments to the normal examination conditions are those whose effects can be described as *substantial*, that is **not** *minor or trivial,* **and** long term. In other words a difficulty has to be demonstrated which *really* affects a candidate during examinations. This may be obvious, as in the case of students with extremely poor literacy skills, or ability to concentrate and so on;

---

[1] JCQ (2010) Access Arrangements, Reasonable Adjustments and Special Consideration, p. vii

or less obvious, but whose effects are nevertheless more than minor or trivial, such as a persisting lack of fluency with some aspects of literacy and language (e.g. word-finding). In such cases a little extra time or a rest break or two would serve to "level the playing field".

Substantial difficulties

Generally, there is no problem identifying candidates with *substantial* or severe difficulties. So long as they have been entered for an appropriate level of examination according to the knowledge and skills they have attained in that subject, it is right and proper to provide them with the help needed to show what they know and can do.

The JCQ regulations define the degree of difficulty with regard to reading and writing skills which they will accept as sufficiently substantial. Since all examinations under the jurisdiction of the JCQ are available nationally to any candidate whatever his age, cognitive ability or background, the same standards regarding 'difficulty in accessing ' must clearly be applied to all candidates. This has been set as one standard deviation below the norm (i.e. below 85) for his age on up-to-date, nationally standardised tests of reading and writing skills.

Centres are sometimes concerned about applying for assistance for candidates with poor literacy skills who would not necessarily be diagnosed as having a 'Specific Learning Difficulty' such as dyslexia. Students who have not developed functional reading and writing skills in their first language, whatever the cause (e.g. ill-health, prolonged absenteeism) still qualify for assistance with reading and writing so long as there is sufficient "evidence of need". In these circumstances there is no need for the *cause* of a student's difficulty in learning to be identified.

In addition, candidates who have problems coping under standard examination conditions due to other conditions such as Autistic Spectrum Disorders (ASD), Emotional/Behavioural Difficulties (EBD), or Attention Deficit Disorder (ADD) can also have adjustments made, appropriate to their needs, so long as these are selected from the "menu" of access arrangements available.

Is the difficulty long-term?

Unless a candidate has an *acquired* learning difficulty (due to injury or illness), the difficulty will be due to a *developmental* disorder. It follows, therefore, that there will be a consistent history of difficulty and delay with the acquisition and development of age appropriate basic skills. The JCQ regulations therefore state that both a history of need and a history of provision are required to support decisions allowing access arrangements.

It is recognised, however, that there are candidates whose learning difficulties may not become very noticeable until curricular demands exceed their capacity to cope comfortably with their studies. In some cases – and this is often found in older students in FE – their learning difficulties may not have been recognised as such when they were younger.

Furthermore, there may be no history of learning support in school for a variety of reasons ranging from shortage of resources to a reluctance on the part of the student to accept such help. Extra tuition may have been provided privately.

However, the vast majority of candidates embarking on GCSE or GCE "A" level courses in schools, who require access arrangements, are expected to have a well-documented history of SEN and learning support.

Borderline Cases

We now come to the thorny issue of what might be considered "minor" or even "trivial" difficulties in terms of their effects on examination performance. Candidates in this category will not be eligible for actual assistance during exams, such as readers or scribes, but only for small adjustments of extra time or a rest break or indeed possibly no adjustment at all.

Unlike the criteria for those with substantial difficulties, the benchmarks for allowing these other arrangements, extra time in particular, are the subject of much debate and on occasions, dispute (see Dolman, 2003[2]). The problem is that the candidates in question will generally have, by definition, literacy skills within the normal range and so are difficult for Centre staff to separate out. Many SENCOs struggle with the issue of candidates who expect extra time because they have an SpLD (diagnosed by a Psychologist or a Specialist Teacher) and yet their literacy skills are every bit as good as those of many other students.

The key to solving this problem is to consider speed of working measures to see if, and to what degree, students are affected in exam situations by specific processing difficulties or a difficulty in either reading or writing speed. (See Chapter 8)

Let us consider some common scenarios:

- A candidate with a long history of specific learning difficulties has, through appropriate intervention and hard work, attained age-appropriate literacy skills within the average range and is what is usually referred to as a 'well-compensated' dyslexic. Although he makes spelling mistakes, these are generally minor so his writing is quite readable, and the style and quality of content reflects his knowledge. However, he often has to re-read text several times to access the meaning, and has to consider his spellings to achieve this degree of accuracy. Specialist diagnostic tests during a recent assessment revealed persisting and significant cognitive processing difficulties across a range of measures (i.e. 1 SD below average for his age). Specialist study skills support and **extra time of up to 25%** during exams is recommended.

- A student experienced some minor difficulties with spelling and writing when younger, but had little or no help at primary school as he was not "below average" and coped quite well. However, he is now becoming anxious about his coursework

---

[2] Dolman, E. (2003) *'Access to Assessments and Qualifications – an Incredible Journey'* in Patoss Bulletin Vol. 16, issue 1

and impending exams. At assessment, his reading and spelling are found to be well within the average range but his writing speed is in the low average range and one cognitive processing test result is also just in the below average range. Study skills support, careful monitoring of progress and **10% extra time** during exams is recommended. Monitoring in mock examinations will check this is appropriate.

- A student with no history of difficulties or provision is not living up to the expectations of his parents – or possibly his school. They believe he may do better if he has extra time. At assessment, a statistically significant discrepancy is found between his general underlying ability, which is above average, and his spelling accuracy, although this is age-appropriate and well within the average range. He makes minor errors which do not impair readability. His writing speed is average and his reading is excellent in all respects. A discrepancy is also found between his underlying ability and the results of one 'cognitive processing' test – but none of these fall outside the average range. He is diagnosed as mildly dyslexic but **no extra time** is awarded.

Many SENCOs as well as some contributors to the 'Readers Letters' in the national press will recognise the introduction to the 3rd example and attribute it to a desire to gain unfair advantage by those who can afford to pay for a private assessment. Indeed abuse of the system is perceived as widespread in some quarters where numbers of pupils are suddenly discovered to have dyslexia in Y11! So let us deal with this issue head on.

There is a public perception that having more time to think and write confers advantage, which may well be true for many students. Indeed a study, in which the views of 66 ordinary 'non-disabled' mock GCSE candidates in Y11 were canvassed (Woods 2000[3]), found that

- *71% reported running out of time in at least one examination.*
- *86% believed they could have gained at least one or two extra marks if they had been allowed extra time[3]*

Giving extra time to candidates who do not have an unusual evidence of need for it and for whom such arrangements have not formed part of normal provision during school-based tests and exams constitutes malpractice. Centre staff should be mindful of the fact that they are acting for and on behalf of the ABs with regard to implementation of the JCQ regulations. Both candidate and Centre may pay the cost of failing to adhere to the regulations.

Part of the problem is that there is also a public perception that anyone with a diagnosis of dyslexia is entitled to 25% extra time in public examinations and that the professional who carries out the assessment is the one who makes this decision. This is most emphatically **not** the case. The decision to either grant or apply for access arrangements will always be made by the Centre, guided by an assessment report produced by a psychologist or suitably

---

[3] Woods, K. (2000) *'Assessment Needs in GCSE Examinations: some student perspectives'* in Educational Psychology in Practice, Vol. 16, No. 2 pp131-140

qualified Specialist Teacher *and* the Centre staff's own knowledge of the candidate's needs and normal way of working.

> The crux of the matter is not 'Is the candidate dyslexic?' but if so, 'What are the effects of his difficulties during exams and will any available access arrangements minimise these?'

It is important to note that the ABs do not see it as in any way appropriate to dispute diagnoses made by professionally qualified practitioners – rather to argue that '**evidence of need**' is the key issue.

Is the student who writes fluently but makes minor spelling mistakes, going to make fewer errors if he has more time? Can he proof-read effectively and so correct spelling mistakes during his extra time allowance? (Since it is axiomatic that dyslexics cannot see where they have made mistakes, this seems unlikely!) These are questions that might be answered during a careful specialist assessment.

In contrast, if students are slowed down when writing because they cannot think how to write words they wish to use and spend time choosing others they know how to spell, and have to re-read questions several times more than other students before they have fully understood them, then extra time will clearly be an appropriate adjustment. Again, careful assessment which includes observation of strategies is crucial.

> *In short, although sound evidence of a learning difficulty is required before any access arrangements are considered, this in itself is not enough. The real issue is always 'evidence of need'.*

What does 'up to 25%' mean?

Centres may find it practical to think in terms of either 10% or 25% extra time according to the degree of need. The case histories in Chapter 10 give some further ideas of the range of test results which might be considered and extra time is discussed again in Chapter 8.

The issue of extra time and fairness is one which is often debated. The JCQ takes the view that achievement of the assessment objectives is the key issue and if a genuinely disabled candidate requires a little extra time in which to demonstrate his attainment, he should not be denied the opportunity.

However, it has long been a common experience of many SENCOs that having taken the trouble to arrange extra time for certain candidates, many did not avail themselves of this opportunity. Either they had written all they could on the subject, or did not want to stay behind for social reasons – and in any case they had not been given guidance on how to use the extra half hour or whatever. None of this is sensible or appropriate. Each candidate's needs must be considered *individually* in relation to the demands of the papers he is taking and his own views.

While applications to cover all exams are made through AAO, Centres should consider and note in their files to which exams these arrangements will apply. The candidate must then have guidance and practice in using the access arrangements deemed appropriate in each subject. Whether the candidate can/does use proposed access arrangements to some benefit could be usefully monitored during mock exams.

Communication

A major awareness campaign may be required to fully inform candidates (and their parents) of the JCQ regulations – and the rationale underpinning them. Teacher led discussion and debate amongst students about special needs, disability, fairness and so-on has been found to lead to a more open and manageable attitude in some Centres.

To support this aspect of the Centre's responsibility see Chapter 7 for:
• Guidelines for Subject Teachers and Learning Support Tutors,
• Introductory Information sheet for Candidates
• Introductory Information sheet for Parents

These may be photocopied and used to promote good practice within the Centre.

Summary

Access arrangements during examinations are available to give those candidates with learning difficulties which significantly affect their performance during examinations, fair opportunities to demonstrate what they know and can do in each subject. No allowances can be made for shortcomings in subject specific knowledge and skills – papers are marked positively against *assessment objectives.* Certificates should convey reliable information to employers, further and higher education institutions etc. about the candidate's attainments in each subject. Close adherence to these principles will give confidence to all in the access arrangement process.

4. Notes for Heads of Centres & Governors

Heads of Centres – the Head Teacher of a school or the Principal of a college – share the responsibility with their Governors for correct implementation of JCQ regulations concerning students who may need access arrangements in assessments and examinations. Allocation of adequate funds and informed management are required to operate a comprehensive policy throughout the Centre, and to support staff in meeting the demands of their roles. In particular, the roles of SENCOs / ALS Managers and Specialist Teachers providing assessments have expanded significantly in recent years and so this needs to be taken into account when timetables are drawn up. In addition, all staff who teach and/or provide learning support to examination candidates need to be aware of their responsibilities in this regard.

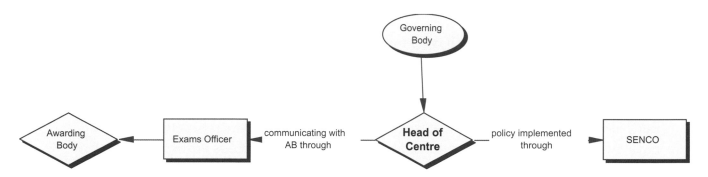

All schools and colleges must comply with the requirements of the Equality Act (2010), which has now superseded the Disability Discrimination Act and the Special Educational Needs and Disability Act. The new Act aims to simplify and update existing law but does not introduce substantial changes[4]. It places duties on education providers to be "**anticipatory**" in their approach to the prevention of discrimination and to make reasonable adjustments in assessments. New statutory Codes of Practice for all sectors of education are to be put before Parliament in the summer of 2011, and the JCQ will amend their regulations if necessary to comply.

You can find useful guidance on the law from The Equality and Human Rights Commission.

The JCQ has, with legal advice, established that Awarding Bodies (AB's) relationships are with Centres rather than candidates. This means that all applications, appeals etc. in connection with access arrangements are the responsibility of the Centre. Neither the JCQ nor the ABs will enter into formal communications directly with candidates or their parents.

It should be noted that the JCQ regulations apply to all candidates with special needs[5] which may affect them during exams; they may or may not have a "disability" as formally defined by the Equality Act. However, not all SENs will impact on examination performance, nor is it always possible to mitigate the effects of a learning difficulty or disability without affecting the assessment objectives. There is a limited "menu" of access arrangements available to meet

---

[4] Equality and Human Rights Commission (2011) http://www.equalityhumanrights.com/
[5] Defined in SEN Code of Practice – DfES (2001)

candidates' needs, and the criteria for permitting them are the same for all Centres across the country. These can and do change from year to year for a variety of reasons and so all Centres must keep up to date with developments when reviewing policy.

To ensure the quality of the access arrangement process Centre policies and practices will need to take account of:

- the early identification of those who may need access arrangements
- the need for training and information for all Centre staff
- the collection of appropriate evidence to meet Inspection requirements
- the appointment of specialist assessment staff.

Identification of Candidates

SENCOs/ALS Managers now have a major commitment with regard to this issue. They need to be given adequate time and up-to-date screening resources to carry out the necessary steps in respect of potential candidates for access arrangements.

Early identification of such candidates should result from their inclusion on the SEN / ALS register, and any information provided by previous Centres of access arrangements permitted during examinations. However, there will always be candidates, who, for various reasons, are not known about, and so screening just before or at the beginning of exam courses is necessary.

This is a particular problem in FE colleges, where large numbers of students enrol late, often for part-time, evening, or one-year courses and do not necessarily have documentation regarding their learning difficulties or provision made in the past.

> *All opportunities to investigate needs prior to the beginning of the course should be taken and individual colleges should consider how this could best be achieved during application, enrolment and initial screening phases.*

Historically, there has been a rush for candidates with learning difficulties to be assessed during the run-up to final exams. There may be a misperception locally that this is still appropriate, but this is not the case.

In all cases, the Centre should initiate early consideration of access arrangements so that candidates, or their parents, do not have to.

Training and Information for all Centre Staff

All subject teachers, lecturers and classroom support staff should be aware of their responsibilities towards candidates with special assessment needs in light of the JCQ regulations. They need to work collaboratively with students and learning support teams, both before and during courses.

- Staff should advise students about the qualifications, options or courses most appropriate for them, in collaboration with learning support staff. Entering a candidate for an examination at a level beyond the limits of his competence/capacity is inappropriate, as is advising him to take a less challenging course solely because of an SpLD. However, Centre policy should not make it difficult for a student to attend a course even if he is unlikely to take the same examination as his peers at the end – or even any exam at all. The educational benefits he will gain simply by participating should not be discounted.

- When courses are underway teaching staff should alert learning support colleagues to any concerns that arise about a particular student so action can be taken, especially those who are not already on the SEN / ALS radar. It is entirely possible, especially in older students that difficulties only emerge as a consequence of more demanding courses, for example during the move to A level or FE courses.

- Staff should also offer practice opportunities in class tests and other assessments for all arrangements awarded. Records of this practice will also usefully contribute to the history of provision evidence required by JCQ Inspectors.

A thorough induction and ongoing professional development programme is needed to ensure all staff are aware of their role and the systems in place in the Centre.

Evidence Requirements

Heads of Centres need to be certain sufficient evidence is available to Inspectors to substantiate arrangements awarded.

For most arrangements candidates must have a formal specialist assessment report concerning their difficulties, to provide sufficiently current "evidence of need". This means a specialist assessment report written within the secondary or FE phase of education for some arrangements, and reports less than 26 months old for others[6]. Only appropriately qualified Specialist Teachers and Psychologists are able to conduct assessments and produce these reports. Not all SENCOs, or those with advanced SEN qualifications, have the required post-graduate level of skills concerning assessment of SpLD to prepare these reports. (See "Specialist Staff" section below.)

---

[6] The different requirements are laid out in the JCQ regulations and discussed in Chapter 6

For all arrangements Centres must also present a history of need, which shows the difficulty is long term and has an impact that is not "minor" or "trivial", and detail the history of provision made *during the course*, where confirmation of the candidate's normal way of working is required. Cases of late identification are noted in Chapter 6, but these would be the exception rather than the rule.

It is of note that while a privately commissioned formal diagnostic assessment report can support an arrangement, the final decision to apply for an access arrangement is made by the Head of Centre who can accept or reject the private report taking into account the current needs of the candidate.

JCQ Inspectors will, when visiting the Centre, ask to see all the supporting evidence. Failure to provide evidence of the required standard, on demand, constitutes malpractice. Centres must not permit access arrangements for which there is insufficient evidence and which have not been approved where needed by the JCQ or relevant Awarding Body.

Specialist Assessment Staff

Since 2007, Heads of Centres are required to take responsibility for delegating the access arrangement assessment task to a professional whose qualifications and experience are fit for purpose. In choosing assessment staff, Heads of Centres must meet JCQ requirements that:

- the rigour of the testing of candidates is maintained
- arrangements are requested only for those with genuine and formally identified needs which reflect their normal way of working within the Centre
- the quality of the reports used to substantiate these arrangements is such that all the required evidence is provided to justify the request being made.

The JCQ recommends that a suitably qualified Specialist Teacher be employed on the Centre staff. If this is not practical a Specialist Teacher from a neighbouring school or college or the Local Authority, or a local independent practitioner, will need to be contracted to conduct the formal assessments. In any case, funds must be set aside and JCQ informed of all Specialist Teachers deployed in your Centre.

Copies of certificates showing specialist assessment qualifications and a rationale for employment for all assessors should be kept in the Centre. This will be available from standard records for those employed within the Centre but will need to be put in place for external professionals.

Assessment Resources

The assessment task is a substantial one and the specialist must have adequate time and up-to-date test resources to carry out all the assessments within normal working hours and to the required standard. As a Head of Centre you will need to consider the likely workload in your Centre and make sufficient provision to meet it.

Qualifications

The JCQ no longer continues to update its list of suitable qualifications for access arrangements assessors, yet Heads of Centres must be able to determine the suitability of staff. The recent Rose Review (2009) - *Identifying and Teaching Children and Young People with Dyslexia and Literacy Difficulties*[7] - has endorsed the SpLD Assessment Practising Certificate (APC) as a useful quality standard for schools in this regard.

The APC was established following the 2005 DfES / SpLD Working Party, and is overseen by the national SpLD Assessment Standards Committee (SASC)[8]. The APC, which is subject to renewal every 3 years, recognises that the holder has relevant and up-to-date knowledge and competence in assessment of SpLDs, as well as a commitment to CPD and a professional code of ethics.

Therefore, Patoss recommends that a Head of Centre wishing to determine if a Specialist Teacher is suitably qualified to assess SpLD students should regard the following as the order of priority in looking at their qualifications. They should hold:

1. a current SpLD Assessment Practising Certificate, **OR**

2. a qualification accredited by the BDA as meeting AMBDA[9] requirements, **OR**

3. a qualification listed on the JCQ website **OR**

4. in the case of assessments for students who are hearing impaired or have moderate learning difficulties, Heads of Centres may wish to consider other qualifications.

We must point out that the JCQ does not require assessors to hold an SpLD APC. However, SASC and its partner organisations including Patoss consider it a model of good practice for Specialist Teachers assessing students with SpLD.

A full breakdown of the set of skills and knowledge recommended for those who assess candidates with learning difficulties is given in Chapter 8, Specialist Teacher Training and Qualifications.

In summary

The provision of an access arrangement is just one part of a Centre's responsibility to students with learning difficulties, but an important one. Best practice in this area will enable

---

[7] DCSF (2009) *Identifying and Teaching Children and Young People with Dyslexia and Literacy Difficulties (Rose Review)* DCSF: London.
[8] SASC is supported by the DfE, DBIS, Patoss, BDA, BPS, Dyslexia Action, HADC and numerous training providers.
[9] Please note it is not a requirement that professionals are 'active' Associate Members of the British Dyslexia Association (BDA) – simply that their qualification met the guidelines for Associate Membership of the BDA (AMBDA) at the time it was completed.

students to have appropriate access to examinations and assessments. It will promote the implementation of a fair system across the country, with the same standards applying in all Centres. Heads of Centres and Governors need to develop, fund, implement and monitor an effective policy in relation to access arrangements, for the sake both of students and the staff who support them.

5. Notes for Exams Officers

As the person responsible for the administration of examinations in your Centre, all of the paperwork relating to access arrangements for candidates with disabilities or learning difficulties will pass through your hands. All applications for access arrangements for GCSEs and GCEs are made through *Access Arrangements Online* (AAO) but paper-based systems remain in place for other qualifications. Regardless of the application method, Centres must manage and maintain thorough supporting paperwork and evidence for all arrangements.

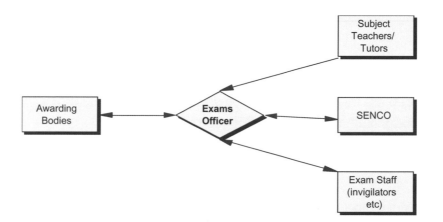

Your precise role in processing the information about each candidate depends on:

*   the nature of the access arrangements required

*   the type of examination being taken

*   the Awarding Body (AB) concerned

*   internal systems within your Centre.

Close liaison with the SENCO / ALS manager and subject and specialist teachers is vital if the process is to work properly. (See Cautionary Tales, Chapter 2)

The JCQ publication *Access Arrangements, Reasonable Adjustments and Special Consideration*, commonly known as the JCQ regulations 'pink book', is the definitive guide for issues relating to access arrangements. It will be at your side at all times!

For GCSE and GCE examinations a *Synopsis of Access Arrangements and Eligibility and/or Evidence Requirements* is provided at the beginning of the JCQ regulations. This shows which arrangements are available, identifying those which must be processed through AAO and those where this is not needed.

Detailed guidance on the arrangements available for Basic and Key Skills, Functional Skills, Entry Level qualifications and Principal Learning Units are given in later chapters of the regulations. You and your SENCO will have to study these carefully as the availability of arrangements, the evidence required and the application process varies.

Exams Officers will also need to take advice from individual ABs who are not part of the JCQ with regard to making applications for certain other qualifications – especially vocational and occupational ones. Each organisation will have its own guidance and systems for management of access arrangements.

Planning for Access Arrangement Applications

Timing

Time spent planning a flow-chart of who should do what and when throughout the year will be time and trouble saved in the long run.

The *Deadlines for Submitting Applications* are stated right at the beginning of the JCQ regulations and these are the dates from which you should work *backwards* to ensure that all the paperwork is completed and processed in good time.

It is especially important that applications for modified papers are made by the deadline.

There is a very useful online Key Dates Calendar currently available through the QCDA[10] website. This lists all the dates in relation to access arrangements and modified papers for the coming academic year and is an invaluable tool for Exams Officers.

In most cases access arrangements should be agreed and in place at the beginning – not at the end – of an examination course, whether the candidate has embarked on a 1 or 2 year course, or indeed any other duration. As these arrangements apply to course-work as well as modules and final exams they need to be agreed in good time.

However, AAO applications can be made at any point as long it is before the examination. Thus if a candidate is identified late into the course, an application for an arrangement can be submitted after the deadline as feedback is instantaneous, although you must be wary as late applications do not allow time for referrals should the request be denied.

This flexibility is not available where a paper application has to be sent to an AB. This must be submitted at least six weeks before the candidate's first exam.

You will most likely be collating and processing applications either during the second part of the summer term preceding the start of the exam course or at the beginning of the autumn term. In FE colleges and 6th forms where many students take 1-year courses, there will be some particular urgency during the autumn term – especially if students have any exams during the winter series. FE college courses may not follow the traditional timing pattern of GCSEs and A levels so it is important to investigate the particular qualifications you offer.

---

[10] Qualifications and Curriculum Development Agency http://www.qcda.gov.uk/ - this agency is closing as part of Government reforms. It is likely that QCDA resources will be re-located but specific details have not been announced at the time of writing.

When planning the Exams Office work you should bear in mind the following steps which need to be taken before you can process the application:

- The SENCO / ALS manager needs time to identify potential candidates, gather the history of their needs and record their current support provision and normal way of working.

- The Specialist Teacher or Psychologist will need to be contacted. They will provide the specialist evidence to support the arrangement and they will need notice and time to carry out each assessment and further time to write up their report. (See "Assessors" below")

- The SENCO then has to decide, with the specialist assessor's guidance, which is the most appropriate arrangement for each exam.

You will need to work very closely with the SENCO, ALS manager and/or Specialist Teacher, and support each other, so everything is in place on time.

Assessors

You will need to submit to the JCQ a list of **all** Specialist Teachers who supply assessments for your Centre, **before** submitting an application based on their work. AAO or JCQ Form 8A should be used for this purpose. Within the AAO system you can use the "Manage Specialist Teacher" facility to add, amend, and view your list of Specialist Teachers.

If a Centre is employing the services of a professional who does not teach in the Centre, they must have been deemed to have suitable qualifications by the Head of Centre and you must notify that person to the JCQ as contracted to work for your Centre.

> Copies of assessors' certificates and a statement outlining the rationale for their appointment from the Head of Centre should be kept in the Centre. This will be available from standard records for those employed within the Centre but files will need to be made for external professionals.

Privately Commissioned Assessors

If a Centre accepts a privately commissioned assessment report from a Psychologist or Specialist Teacher, then there must be a statement on file explaining why. The JCQ state this is not a job for the Examinations Officer, but the Head of Centre who is responsible for giving approval for all assessors. They must decide whether or not to accept the report and in either case state the reasons for doing so.

Making Applications

To determine which route to follow to make your application you must first determine the qualifications concerned.

Which qualifications are the candidates in your Centre seeking?	
Qualification	**Application Method**
GCSE / GCE only	AAO
GCSE / GCE with any "Skill" qualification*	AAO
"Skill" qualifications* only	Paper-based system through AB following JCQ system
Other vocational or occupation qualification	Paper-based system through AB following individual AB system

* "Skill" qualifications are: Basic and Key Skills, Functional Skills, Entry Level Qualifications and Principal Learning Units.

Access Arrangements Online (AAO)

This online tool is available from any JCQ AB secure site and handles all applications for arrangements for GCSE and GCE qualifications. AAO is used for arrangements which previously required formal AB approval and also some arrangements which were previously delegated to the Centre, for example, extra time.

Before making the application you will have to:

Gain the candidates' consent to enter their personal information into AAO to meet data protection requirements. A sample form for this purpose is provided in the JCQ regulations. It should be signed by the candidate and kept on file.

Next, you will have to ensure you have all the evidence from the SENCO / ALS manager and Specialist Teacher – this will probably be:
- a specialist assessment report – check it has been signed by the assessor **PLUS**
- evidence of need and normal way of working.

The JCQ recommends all this evidence is brought together on Form 8, the Application for Access Arrangements, although a Centre-devised alternative which addresses the same key questions is acceptable. This might be a typed statement from the SENCO, attached to a specialist report. It is best to agree a policy on how evidence will be presented with your colleagues in learning support well before you begin each year.

It is worth carefully proof-reading the specialist reports you receive before beginning the application; while online mistakes can be corrected, if you do spot any errors or omissions you will save yourself and your colleagues a good deal of time and trouble.

Using the AAO system

When you begin an application the system prompts you to supply and/or retain on file the required evidence for the arrangements you request. Where arrangements need the results of specialist assessments these have to be directly input to the AAO system.

Where the supplied evidence meets JCQ criteria, approval is usually given on the spot. (See below for when an application is declined.) Make sure to print a copy of the approval.

Finally, inform the SENCO / ALS manager of the AAO outcome and send them a copy of the confirmation so they can inform teaching staff and candidates and make any necessary arrangements for mock examinations, classroom tests or other assessments.

> Clip all the evidence and paperwork together for each candidate and place on file.

If AAO declines an application, or a particularly complex case arises, you may make an online **AB Referral**. You may be asked to send further evidence and the AB will consider the circumstances before making a decision – you will need to liaise with your SENCO here. However, before requesting a referral you should very carefully check the JCQ regulations, as any application which does not meet the published guidance will not be granted.

Please note that if arrangements need approval they must NOT be put in place until confirmed.

Paper-based Applications

Where the qualification is offered by an AB who works within the JCQ but it is **not covered by AAO** – essentially all the "Skills" qualifications - you will need to follow essentially the same process as above, although the need for the data protection statement is removed.

In this case, however, you **must** complete JCQ Form 8 and use the paper-based process for those arrangements requiring AB approval, e.g. readers and scribes. These must be submitted to the AB at least 6 weeks before the candidate's first exam.

Where arrangement approvals are delegated to the Centre *and* evidence is required, e.g. up to 25% extra time, we recommend for consistency that you record the evidence on Form 8, but a Centre-devised alternative is acceptable. These Centre-granted arrangements **must** be recorded on **JCQ Form 9**.

See the JCQ regulations for full lists of arrangements and relevant reporting requirements.

Remember, if a candidate is taking a GCSE or GCE with some "Skill" qualifications their application through AAO will suffice.

Applications for Modified Papers

Applications for modified papers should always be processed for each examination series by the deadline in the JCQ regulations. Please note these may be earlier than the date of entry. It may also be useful for Exams Officers to check that the modified paper requests and actual examination entries made to an AB match. Where a mismatch has occurred or amendments have subsequently been made to a candidate's entries, thus impacting on the order(s) for modified papers, the AB must be contacted as soon as possible. This is important, as AAO is not linked to AB entry systems. (See Cautionary Tales, Chapter 2)

Arrangements Awarded by the Centre

Arrangements awarded by the Centre, for qualifications covered by the JCQ, need no formal application or prior approval, and no specialist assessment evidence is required for Inspectors, although information regarding the normal way of working of all the candidates who have them will still be noted in Centre SEN / ALS records.

Always check the annually updated JCQ regulations for the up-to-date list of Centre-awarded arrangements. The arrangements that fall into this category most commonly needed by students with SpLD are:

- Use of a word processor
- Use of coloured overlays
- Prompter
- Read Aloud
- Use of OCR (Optical Character Recognition) scanners
- Transcript (from September 2011 only)

This is not an exhaustive list! In total there are 11 Centre-awarded arrangements rising to 13 from September 2011.[11]

Exams Officers certainly need to be aware of requests for such arrangements so they can make appropriate plans for resources, rooms, invigilators etc. Many of these arrangements can be given if they represent the candidate's normal way of working within the Centre and they do not give the candidate an unfair advantage over their peers – the underlying principles of access arrangements still apply even though no formal application is made.

Note on use of Word Processors: You must ensure that any word processor to be used in the exam is set up according to JCQ regulations. If the candidate wishes to use features such as voice-recognition software, predictive text and/or a spell check the Centre must apply for the use of a scribe.

---

[11] Both use of a transcript and use of a bilingual dictionary without any extra time will become Centre-awarded arrangements from September 2011

JCQ Inspectors who visit Centres during examinations may ask to see the evidence relating to any candidate who has access arrangements. Failure to retain the required documentation is regarded as malpractice and carries significant consequences.

Vocational and Occupational Qualifications

For all those qualifications which do not come under the JCQ, Exams Officers should investigate the instructions of the AB concerned; some of these qualifications have subject specific issues relating to access arrangements. All the above guidance will have to be re-considered to check if it applies to this AB.

These ABs are likely to have their own regulations, systems, paperwork and notification deadlines in place to approve access arrangements - research is needed to ensure they are followed so candidates' needs are met in a timely fashion.

The process for applying for an arrangement for this type of qualification is generally a paper based one. Again, the AB will allow Centres to make the decision regarding some types of arrangement. For arrangements requiring approval, applications should be sent to the AB **at least six weeks before the first exam** that the student will be taking.

Setting up the Arrangements

Accommodation

Separate rooms are clearly ideal for candidates who are permitted to read aloud to themselves or are supported by readers, scribes, prompters etc. However, each room will require a separate invigilator. If this is not possible, adequate space with office dividers in the examination room can work well, but care must be taken to ensure that other candidates are not disturbed.

It is generally more convenient for candidates permitted extra time to sit in a group rather than in number order, so they are not distracted by the majority leaving the room. Better still, a separate room (with invigilator) should be booked, if possible.

Don't forget, the smaller exam rooms where students with access arrangements are working will need all the usual signs; a white board or similar placed in the corridor outside these additional rooms for exams will reinforce the "Do not enter" signs on the door.

Invigilators and Supporting Staff

Training and support for these colleagues **well in advance** of the examination is extremely valuable so they are aware of their responsibilities, the function and limitations of their role, and the overarching goals of access arrangements.

Liaise with your SENCO to check your support team of readers etc. have established a suitable way of working with the candidate well before the exam. Last minute introductions to people acting as readers and scribes do not serve candidates well!

The information all supporting colleagues need divides into "general" and "on-the-day".

General information

It is advisable to prepare notes for every category of support staff – readers, scribes, practical assistants, ICT technicians, transcribers, prompters, sign language interpreters, oral language modifiers – showing precisely what they must and must not do during the exams. You can download the relevant notes from the JCQ regulations, which have been agreed and checked by the JCQ and its advisors. If you prepare your own notes you must be certain to incorporate exactly what the JCQ has advised in their regulations, and ensure they include the most up-to-date guidance. Make sufficient copies for each person. You could laminate them for durability, but if the rules change this is a job that will have to be done again!

Go through these notes with your team of supporting staff to ensure they all know what they can do and what they must *not* do. It may be worth re-iterating these on the day of the exam. To supplement the full notes, the JCQ regulations includes a memory aid for readers, scribes, oral language modifiers and sign language interpreters which you can photocopy.

It is helpful to prepare a matching information sheet for the candidates, so that they know exactly what the supporter can and cannot do for them during the exam.

A complete timetable showing all the candidates with access arrangements, which room they will be in (book the rooms first!), the name of the supporter, and start & finish times for each day is extremely useful and should be displayed somewhere prominent in the staff room. Clearly candidates with access arrangements need all this information individually as well – where they will be, who will be with them, times etc.

On the day of the examination

A robust system is required for distributing the papers from the main examination room to all the separate rooms at the beginning of each exam.

All invigilators need to know which candidates are permitted extra time and how much (10%, 25% or granted %), as well as any approved supervised rest breaks.

Some arrangements require cover sheets to be attached to exam scripts; pre-populated forms are generated by AAO. Give this sheet to staff **prior to the exam** and ask them to complete and sign it. Cover sheets are required at present for the following arrangements but do check the up-to-date regulations:

- scribe
- practical assistant
- sign language interpreter
- oral language modifier
- word processor (cover sheet available on JCQ website)
- transcript (from Sept. 2011 cover sheet will need to be downloaded from JCQ website)

If approved access arrangements are not used, attach the cover sheet to the candidate's work in the usual way, but mark it clearly: Arrangement **NOT USED**.

Completing the Process

These are some important things to wrap up the process.

- Collect and review feedback sheets from invigilators (see Chapter 6) so you can evaluate the effectiveness of all arrangements.
- Check your paperwork and be sure all required evidence is on file supporting all access arrangements that were granted.
- Make sure your team of Specialist Teacher assessors is lined up for next year and add the name and qualifications of any new Specialist Teachers to Form 8A through AAO.

Then you will be ready for next year!

But remember:

> AT THE BEGINNING OF EACH ACADEMIC YEAR, CHECK THE NEW ISSUE OF THE JCQ GUIDANCE AND NOTE ANY CHANGES

JCQ Website: www.jcq.org.uk.

It is useful to check this site during the year for any amendments. Copies of all guidance and forms are available on the site.

6. Notes for SENCOs and ALS Managers

As the school SENCO or college ALS Manager you have a pivotal role in supporting students with SpLD, in managing exam arrangements and ensuring this is just one element in their ongoing learning support.

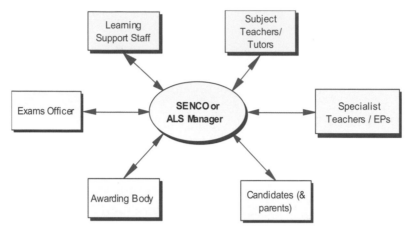

You will need to:

- organise the early identification of potential candidates
- co-ordinate the access arrangements application process
- manage a team of support staff, possibly employed both inside and outside your Centre
- keep up-to-date with JCQ regulations and play your part in ensuring your Centre meets its legal obligations as well as its role in delivering a fair examination system
- liaise with candidates, parents/carers, subject teachers, Exams Officers and your Head of Centre.

A clear plan is going to be needed to cover all these issues!

This chapter will cover briefly the basic principles that apply to all Centres, and it includes additional notes for FE. Caroline Read considers further dedicated advice for school SENCOs in the next chapter.

Identification of Potential Candidates

Students who may need access arrangements should be identified **at the beginning** of their examination courses. Thus, an early and effective screening programme is needed. This is likely to be a substantial under-taking. You will then need to arrange follow-up specialist assessments for those who need them.

Your screening programme will include gathering existing information about the candidate - if they are moving up from earlier years in your Centre that should be straightforward. If they are transferring from elsewhere it might be more difficult, especially in FE. You could take opportunities at **application**, **interview**, **enrolment** and **tutorial** stages to ask candidates about any past support or access arrangements. Make sure you consider data protection and confidentiality issues when asking for (or sending) information about students – you will need to get permission to do so.

The screening programme in FE is likely to be more compressed than in a school and often can only be implemented during the first week of the course, although it may be possible during course preview days. It is very difficult to screen effectively across the enormous range of learners attending FE but Morris & White[12] suggest an informal way to do this effectively without embarrassing or patronising anyone.

This early identification is needed as **arrangements apply throughout the course** - to modules and course work, class tests, mock exams and controlled assessments as well as formal, external examinations. Use of the arrangement throughout the course establishes it as the student's normal way of working, a JCQ requirement.

You will also need to consider
- any candidates studying at another Centre – it is the responsibility of the candidates' home Centre to make sure support is in place.
- any candidates following alternative curricula, studying part-time, or following work-based or outreach programmes – a particular issue in FE

Group Testing

The use of group or computer based testing of either underlying cognitive abilities or literacy skills is extremely useful, saving time and helping to cope with the workload, while giving you valuable information about your candidates. Some caution is needed however:

- If your screening system includes group cognitive ability testing you should be aware that results from such tests may misrepresent students with SpLDs due to weak literacy skills, the style of the test materials and response sheet, processing speed weaknesses, attention or concentration problems
- Computer based tests can be measuring keyboard or IT skills rather than underlying ability or literacy skills!
- Motivation to complete literacy or ability tests may affect results – especially self-directed online tests. The temptation for students to simply click "finish" when they see others leaving can be significant for some; older candidates in FE might find such literacy screening materials demeaning.
- Group tests must carefully match the requirements of JCQ evidence demands if they are to be used for access arrangements.

---

[12] Morris, K and White, A (2005) *Further and Higher Education* in Backhouse, G and Morris, K (Eds) Dyslexia? Assessing and Reporting – the Patoss Guide, Hodder Murray: London

Late Identification of Candidates

Late diagnosis of difficulties does occur, but this should be the exception; even the best screening systems might miss one or two students whose needs come to light during the course. In this case, you can still apply for an access arrangement, painting a picture of the student's profile using specialist assessment evidence and their current needs. You can then confirm that all arrangements will become "normal".

Early Communication

In both school and college environments a key issue is student (and parent) **awareness of the rationale for the JCQ regulations**, as well as an alert and informed community of teaching staff. A good deal of misinformation and hearsay still exists about access arrangements – who may be eligible for them, who can prepare the necessary reports and when these have to be done. Information for candidates, parents and subject teachers, tutors and lecturers (see Chapter 7) may be copied and distributed within your institution (on eye-catching coloured paper!) to aid wider understanding.

Prior to induction, details about learning support and the possibility of access arrangements can be included in school and college information and mentioned at open days – indeed any opportunity to share information with new students.

Assessment

Where screening suggests an arrangement might be needed, a further assessment will be required in most cases. To manage the load you might prioritise based on the timescale of examinations.

You will likely need to gather both general and specialist evidence so we will address these in turn.

General Evidence Requirements

History of Need and Provision

As SENCO / ALS manager you will need to gather some details of what has gone before for this learner, and make note of the current steps being taken to support them. This will all help to paint a picture of the student.

Centres are sometimes concerned that where no history exists they cannot make an arrangement – this is not necessarily the case. As noted in Chapter 3 it is anticipated that most will have an established history but some learners may have coped independently thus far, or for others, needs might not have been recognised. If your early screening programme suggests a need, this data can be included in the background information of your application, perhaps with qualitative information from the student about their difficulties to support your specialist assessment evidence.

Normal Way of Working

> It is the Centre's responsibility to decide if an application is justified under the JCQ regulations. Centre staff must base their decision on evidence of **current** need. How does the candidate normally work? How is he supported? How does he cope with internal assessments or mock examinations?

One of the most efficient ways to establish a normal way of working is to observe and record how arrangements are used in **mock exams** through a feedback sheet – a sample is included at the end of this chapter[13]. (It includes issues to do with accommodation and information for staff involved and should therefore be made available to the Exams Officer.) The information gathered is very useful to staff and students.

If this feedback is collected during the mock exams by all colleagues invigilating and assisting:

- Any problems experienced by staff can be sorted out before the final exams and avoided in subsequent years.
- Staff will be able to discuss how (whether) the access arrangements were used with each candidate and make final decisions as to what is the most effective adjustment. Candidates permitted extra time in mock exams might be provided with a different colour pen to use during the additional time allowance. The use made of this adjustment can then be monitored and evaluated.

This is particularly useful for learners whose specialist report was written before Year 9 and SENCOs / ALS managers wish to establish that the arrangements recommended remain useful.

You might also need to gather **information from teachers** about classroom practice in order to make the most effective decision for the student – this will be especially the case where there are no mock exams. The compilation of information from teaching and support staff can then provide normal way of working evidence. In FE this should be done over the first term, to balance the need to allow staff sufficient time to get to know their students against the need to decide on arrangements early.

You could develop a quick checklist, with Yes/No answers, to suit your Centre to send to busy teaching staff to confirm some everyday questions and give them an opportunity to give you "any other useful information or comments". You might consider questions such as:

---

[13] From an idea suggested by Roger Lewis, SpLD Base Team Leader, Francis Combe School and Community College, Watford, Herts.

Does your student …

- Regularly need extra time to complete work – perhaps they read, write, copy or take notes very slowly?
- Need extra time in mock exams or class tests?
- Regularly need individual help with reading
- Regularly need help with writing
- Normally use a word processor to take notes in class
- Normally use a word processor in class tests and mock exams
- Very often need to be prompted to maintain attention on task
- Regularly receive help from a learning support assistant

Once you are confident you have the right information about a candidate, you can put a clear statement in regard to normal way of working in your file.

Specialist Assessment

The specialist assessment is an investigation of a student's difficulty in learning carried out by an appropriately qualified Specialist Teacher or Psychologist. They will make recommendations in regard to access arrangements. The arrangements required will have a significant bearing on the additional **evidence** you need to collect, the **paperwork** you complete and the **staff** you need.

This assessment may well be the first time the student has had a formal investigation of their difficulties, or it may be a review of progress. Whichever it is, a confirmation that learning difficulties exist is necessary, *although not sufficient*, to make the application.

It should be recalled that **a diagnosis of a *Specific* Learning Difficulty, such as dyslexia, is not required for access arrangements** but teachers and students may "need to know" and teachers and learning support staff will appreciate guidance on how best to support a particular student – these are questions a fuller assessment could address. What is crucial here is not the label but the effect of the difficulty on performance in exams and assessments. (Equally, where a diagnosis of an SpLD does exist, this is not sufficient of itself to award an arrangement.)

Specialist Evidence Requirements

Access arrangements for candidates with learning difficulties
(Applicable to 2010/11 regulations)

- Those who need a reader, a scribe, an oral language modifier or extra time of more than 25%, must have a specialist assessment **carried out within 26 months of the final exam.**

- For extra time of up to 25% a specialist assessment carried out at any point **within secondary education or FE** is necessary and sufficient.

However, a further group of arrangements exist where **no specialist evidence** is required. These are listed in the JCQ regulations but those most commonly relevant to students with learning difficulties are use of a **word processor**[14], **a prompter, read aloud facility, and use of coloured overlays**. From September 2011 this will also include a **transcript**. (*Please note this is not an exhaustive list.*)

Assessment for post-16 students

To meet best practice guidelines Patoss recommends that wherever possible a full diagnostic assessment meeting the DfES 2005 / SpLD Working Party Guidelines is undertaken for a 16+ student who plans to go to HE. This way the student can avoid further assessment and use the report to provide evidence of their disability. If this is not possible, you should make sure they understand that further assessment will be necessary and give advice about making early applications for support, Disabled Students Allowances (DSA) and access arrangements at University.

For those FE colleges supporting students taking HE courses their assessments **must** meet these Guidelines for the student to secure DSA funding for support. Final decisions about access arrangements in these cases are guided by the policies of the awarding HE Institution.

Recording Evidence

JCQ Form 8 - Application for Access Arrangements: the Profile of Learning Difficulties

Although many applications are processed through AAO the JCQ recommends that all the relevant supporting information be collated on **Form 8** or a **Centre-devised equivalent that addresses the same key questions.**

To help our discussion of the evidence requirements we will assume that Form 8 will be retained, which is the practice in many Centres. You will find a copy on the JCQ website.

The process of recording evidence is started and completed in the Centre.

- Section A of Form 8 must be completed by you or a colleague **before** the candidate has his formal assessment. This records history of need – essentially the background information – and the past and current provision of support. It must also include a statement confirming "normal way of working".

---

[14] Please also see Chapter 8 in regard to the use of word processors.

- Completion of Section B is also a Centre responsibility and is done **after** the assessment report has been received and discussed. This is the arrangement recommendation.

Section C of JCQ Form 8 ... *sometimes also known as "the diagnostic report"[15]*.

Where a specialist assessment is required, a copy of the results must be kept in the Centre. The JCQ recommends results are recorded using Section C of Form 8. Specialist assessors directly employed by the Centre may take an alternative route and use a Centre-devised equivalent to record their results, as long as it addresses the same key questions. External professionals should use Form 8 or agree a format with you. This is to ensure that information is provided to Exams Officers in a familiar, easily accessible and consistent way to allow them to complete JCQ requirements and, equally, for the ease of JCQ inspectors.

> The Form 8 and any other specialist reports and evidence of need, with a statement of normal way of working, relating to each candidate must be collated and placed on file and made available for inspection (see Chapter 5). **Failure to produce the required evidence on demand constitutes malpractice**.

Deciding on arrangements

The **general principles** which apply to GCSE and A level examinations also apply to Basic and Key Skills, Functional Skills, Entry Level qualifications, Principal Learning Units and vocational qualifications – all covered by the JCQ. The arrangements available for these latter qualifications are not all exactly the same as those for GCSEs and A levels, so a thorough check of the annually published JCQ regulations will be needed. If your Centre offers qualifications granted by ABs outside the JCQ slightly different arrangements and application systems might apply.

As the Head of Centre has likely delegated responsibility for day-to-day operation of access arrangements to you, you share the duty to maintain the integrity and validity of the examination process. The JCQ places requirements on Centres to ensure:
- The rigour of testing of candidates is maintained
- The quality of reports is such that all required evidence is provided to justify requests
- Arrangements are recommended only for those with genuine and formally identified needs which reflect their normal way of working within the Centre.

The specialist assessor will advise but as SENCO / ALS Manager you should also be aware of the range of arrangements available so you can consider the best approach for each candidate. You might ask the following questions:

---

[15] Please note this "diagnostic report" is not the same as a "full diagnostic report" which gives a formal diagnosis of an SpLD. See Figure 8.2 page 73.)

Reading Skills

- Is "read aloud" a good independent option for those who don't want/qualify for an individual reader?
- Is he very familiar with using a computer reader? Does he need to have his own writing read back to him? If so how will this be achieved?
- Would access to a reader in a small group be most effective? This can be useful where the candidate does not need constant support. However, if the candidate has to put up his hand to ask for a word to be read you must ask if he would be confident enough to do so in front of his peers and thus gain full benefit from the arrangement. This is only useful in very small groups where readers are working at a similar level and should not be considered a standard practice for those with very substantial reading difficulties. **Please recall, that access to a reader in a group requires the same level of evidence as an individual reader.**

Writing Skills

- Would a little extra time and / or a word processor mean he could complete his writing independently instead of using scribe?
- Does he prefer to type or handwrite?
- Is he very familiar with voice input software? If not, it should not be used.
- Is a transcript better? The candidate might better express his ideas when writing by hand and so the transcript would be a preferred option over a word processor or scribe.

How much extra time?

In all cases the JCQ asks that consideration is given to a supervised rest break instead of extra time. This would normally apply to students whose difficulty is not with speed of working but with concentration or attention, stress, physical difficulties and so-on, where a short break from the exam would be a much better option than having to stay even longer in the already stressful or painful exam situation.

Options for extra time are
- up to 25% - usually thought of as either 10% or 25% although this is not fixed – and
- over 25%.

Awards of up to 25% are available for those who have a Statement of SEN or scores for reading and/or writing speed and processing difficulties in the below average range. In *exceptional* circumstances some flexibility is allowed for those with processing speeds in the low average range. See Chapter 8 for further discussion. Awards over 25% require more substantial difficulties.

Staff

Specialist Assessors

For the sake of clarity, the roles of SENCO and appropriately qualified Specialist Teacher have been differentiated here. It is often the case that the SENCO and/or a colleague are qualified to carry out the required formal assessments of learning difficulties. In these (ideal) circumstances, all the work connected with access arrangements can be carried out within the Centre including discussions about individual candidates. Sufficient time must be allowed for specialist staff to conduct tests and write up reports.

Should there be a need to contract out the work due to shortage of time or suitably qualified staff, the ideal solution is for independent practitioners or Local Authority staff – whether qualified Psychologists or Specialist Teachers – to carry out the assessments at the Centre. As well as facilitating proper collaboration, this allows an economical approach as some tests can be administered to groups – although all the students will need to be seen individually as well.

See Chapter 8, page 67 for guidance on the appropriate qualifications for these assessors.

Please note that those without specialist qualifications – learning support assistants for example - cannot conduct tests to support access arrangements. For data to be used the specialist has to sign to confirm she has administered the tests herself.

Private Assessments

Please see the notes on privately commissioned assessment reports in Chapter 5 page 39 and FAQ 7, page 120. Difficult situations sometimes arise due to the expectations of candidates or their parents on the basis of such reports. It is hoped that such situations will occur rarely if Centres take initiatives to promote awareness of both the "letter and spirit" of the regulations, such that all involved are aware of the need to work collaboratively and the need to adhere to the regulations.

Exam Support Staff

You will wish to collaborate with your Exams Officer on the training of all those adults who are engaged to support candidates in exams. They will need to know about the rationale for access arrangements and what they can and cannot do in exams.

It is very important that candidates are introduced to staff who will work with them well before the exam and that they have ample opportunity to practise using the arrangements they have been given.

Informing Candidates and Staff

Having done all this work to investigate and assess need it is important that you have robust systems in place to inform everyone involved of the outcome in good time.

- A candidate needs to know what he has been awarded in which subjects
- Subject staff need to know what to offer in class tests and assessments
- Exams Officers must agree with you detailed plans in regard to need for extra rooms, invigilators, staff and resources, especially word processors.

Some Centres ask candidates to sign a declaration which indicates they are aware of and are in agreement with the arrangements which are planned.

You will probably also find that not all candidates want an access arrangement – even when they qualify for one and you think it a valid and useful adjustment. You would be well advised to ask these candidates to sign a declaration as well to confirm that they have had an opportunity to discuss possible arrangements and have declined them.

Learning Support not just Access Arrangements

The co-ordination of an effective access arrangement programme is a complex task, which will doubtless take a good deal of your time. However, the access arrangement should only be one part of the school or college's support for the student. As a SENCO or ALS Manager, working with the Specialist Teacher, you are in an excellent position to suggest good ways forward to help the learner improve their skills and gain more independence and the access arrangement assessment is an excellent point to begin that process.

Staff Feedback Sheet – Access Arrangements

Please complete this after each exam during which you have supported a candidate with access arrangements & return it as soon as possible to ....

Your comments will help us to support the student effectively and deal with any administrative shortcomings in future exam sessions.

Student	Date
Exam	End of year module End of year Mock Public exam Other (specify)

This student was allowed:
 	
   10% extra time
 	
   25% extra time
 	
   Reader
 	
   Scribe
 	
   Bilingual dictionary
 	
   Prompter
 	
   Practical Assistant
 	
   Other (specify)
	S/he used the arrangement
	
	   Well
	
	   Quite well
	
	   Not very well
	
	   Not at all
	
	S/he appeared
	
	   Calm & on task
	
	   Anxious
	
	   Other (specify)

Any comments /suggestions regarding future exam arrangements for this student? Any other comments? E.g. implications for revision

Room number	Did you have all the information & resources you needed?

The room was:
 	
   Quiet / Mostly quiet / Noisy
 	
   Well lit / Badly lit
 	
   Too hot / Too cold / Stuffy
 	
   Other (specify)
	Guidance sheets
	   Cover sheet
	   Spare equipment
	   Signs for doors & corridors
	   Other (specify)

Any other comments/suggestions
Your name:

7. The SENCO's Year

by Caroline Read

Access Arrangements Online

Since September 2008 the method for making applications for access arrangements for GCSE and GCE 'A' level have changed from the requirement for paper applications for most arrangements to the Access Arrangements Online (AAO) system. The system can be accessed through any JCQ awarding body website.

Whilst the JCQ regulations do publish deadlines for applications (the dates of which coincide with the final date for the order of exam papers) these are 'soft' deadlines. With the online system applications can be made at any stage leading up to the first exam. However, if applications are left too late, the Centre runs the risk of having an application turned down, meaning there may not be enough time to make a referral to an awarding body for the case to be considered. It is, therefore, good practice to work towards applications being ready by early October.

Please note that the application dates for Modified Papers should still be adhered to as the process of producing the required papers is time consuming for the awarding bodies.

Centres should make it a priority to agree a timeline for screening, testing and administration, which will work within the Centre as well as taking into account the JCQ requirements for evidence to be collated and the regulations regarding deadlines.

Ideally the first raft of applications should be made by 4th October. For students taking modular examinations in November, December or January this is most likely to be in year 10. Assessments for students needing a Reader, Scribe, Oral Language Modifier (OLM) or more than 25% extra time must have been carried out within 26 months of the **final** exam. Therefore, there is a window between early May and early October to carry out assessments, complete reports and make applications. (Some students may take modular exams in year 9, in which case the timeline below will need to be adapted with this in mind).

The following timetable for screening, testing and administration is suggested:

APRIL
- **Consider which students may need access arrangements from information already in the Centre.**

For example:
- the SEN register or equivalent
- students with a Statement of SEN
- those who have had access arrangements previously e.g. for National Curriculum Tests at Key Stage 2, or GCSEs if they are approaching A level
- those who have replied positively to a question on an application or information form asking if they may have any examination access needs or disabilities

N.B. It is important to have a clear system whereby subject tutors and teaching assistants can inform SEN staff of students who may need support. This may require training for staff so they know what arrangements are available and for whom.

If any students require Modified Papers, evidence should be sought now, as applications for these papers for November modules must be made through Access Arrangements Online by 20th September.

MAY / JUNE
   – **Administer tests to groups of candidates as a screening process**

Centres with good systems of communication in place will be aware of most of the candidates with special needs. Screening tests should bring few surprises. However, group screening tests will occasionally identify a student whose need has been overlooked, and will also save time administering some tests on an individual basis.

Group tests for year 9 students can take place from early May onwards (to fit in with the requirement for specialist assessments to be within 26 months of the final exam). Some Centres use the main hall to screen the whole of year 9 after GCSEs have finished, while the examinations desks are still out.

If the Specialist Teacher or Psychologist who will be completing JCQ Form 8 Section C (the profile of learning difficulties) can be present to administer the test to the group, the screening tests can be used as evidence in this section, if appropriate. This will save time re-testing later. If they are not present this test data cannot be used. This is because the professional completing this section must sign to confirm that he/she carried out all the tests.

JULY / AUGUST / EARLY SEPTEMBER
   – **Mark screening tests and set up a file of evidence and information for all students who may need access arrangements.**

A pro forma sheet (see an example in Chapter 8, page 98) with a summary of the student's scores and personal information placed at the front of each file will make analysis of his need easier and will save time when Form 8 is completed.

SEPTEMBER
• For students needing Modified Papers, apply through Access Arrangements Online.

• Earmark as a priority all students who are likely to need access to a Reader, Scribe, Oral Language Modifier or more than 25% extra time and who will be sitting modules between November and January.

- GCE 'A' level students who had access arrangements for GCSEs, whose report is now out of date, will need to have the relevant tests updated. Most applications will have expired by year 12 as permission is only granted for a maximum of 26 months.

- It is also important to note there may be a need for re-assessment when candidates move from one qualification type to another as the demands of the specification will be different, and this may give rise to the need for alternative access arrangements.

A Specialist Teacher or Psychologist needs to complete other tests as necessary with these students, some in groups (e.g. a number of students may need a spelling test, in which case administer a test to a group to save time) but most individually.

Also …

A student who does not already have a specialist report or a formal Statement of Special Educational Need but appears to need up to 25% extra time will need an assessment by a suitably qualified Specialist Teacher or Psychologist.

Extra Time

At this stage it is worth considering students who may need up to 25% extra time. Candidates with a report from a Specialist Teacher or Psychologist completed since the start of Year 7, confirming the existence of a learning difficulty, will only need updated evidence that the need for extra time still exists, as long as the existing evidence still meets the current criteria. See Chapter 8.

Assessment scores must be presented with other evidence to "paint a picture" of the student's need. This might take a wide variety of forms but is likely to be sampled from observations of mock exam performance, IEPs, a compilation of teaching / learning support staff reports showing clear need for extra time or results of group screening tests.

All evidence should be kept on file with the specialist report to evidence the student's normal working practice, in case a JCQ Inspector asks to see evidence during a visit.

SENCOs should be aware assessments used as evidence for up to 25% extra time do not need to be within 26 months of the final exam, though AAO will only grant permission for 26 months starting from the date of application rather than the date of assessment.

It is important to take time during individual testing to discuss with the student what access arrangements he feels are appropriate for him. A policy decision should be made within the Centre as to who is responsible for having this discussion and how to deal with students who are adamant that they do not want access arrangements. Consider producing a letter explaining that the student has been informed that he may be eligible for specific access arrangements but has elected not to accept them. The student should sign this letter and parents must be informed. Keep the letter on file in case of repercussions after the student has left the Centre.

- All candidates given access arrangements need to sign a 'Data Protection Notice' giving their permission for their data to be entered on AAO.

- The appointed person collates all the required information to complete Section A of JCQ Form 8, or a Centre-devised equivalent, giving history of need and provision.

Discussion between the SENCO and Specialist Teacher or Psychologist is essential at this stage (unless, of course, the one person carries out both the role of coordinator and assessor).

Though it is the Centre's responsibility to make the application for the appropriate access arrangements, the decision as to what should be applied for should be made on the basis of:
- the findings of the Specialist Teacher or Psychologist
- the Centre's knowledge of the student
- his normal way of working
- the requirements of the subjects he is taking.

For this reason, applications based entirely on a recommendation by an independent Specialist Teacher or Psychologist who has no knowledge of the student's needs in school, are unacceptable. If a Centre does decide to accept a report carried out by an independent assessor (which must have a **clear** indication of evidence of need) a typed statement stating why the report has been accepted must be attached.

- The Specialist Teacher or Psychologist should complete Section C of Form 8, and the SENCO Section B of JCQ Form 8. There is now sufficient information for an application to be submitted through AAO. Historically the Exams Officer has been responsible for this part of the process, but increasingly, with the advent of AAO the Learning Support or Special Needs department are making the applications online.

OCTOBER
- **Make applications for access arrangements through AAO.**

- Where the appropriate evidence of need and other relevant criteria can be met the system will approve the application immediately, but if applications don't fully meet all the criteria they will not be approved. In this case Centres should refer to the JCQ regulations to check whether the application meets the required criteria.

- Where an application is not approved and the Centre believes there is a good evidence to justify the arrangement, Centres may decide to refer these cases for consideration by a member of staff at the appropriate awarding body. Well over 95 percent of applications can be processed through AAO, but a small percentage of applications do need further investigation beyond the rules based decisions offered by the online system. A referral to the awarding body can be done through Access Arrangements Online and replies will be sent by email.

- If the application is for multiple arrangements AAO will approve or refuse all the arrangements, the system cannot split approval. Where Centres believe that one of the arrangements does meet the required criteria it is acceptable to reapply for that arrangement. There is no problem with a student having more than one entry on AAO as long as there is a genuine reason for this.

- Please note that Centres no longer need to list the candidate's subject entries at this stage; this information is only required for Modified Paper applications or if a referral to an awarding body is required because an application for access arrangements has not been approved.

The SENCO should now concentrate on students who may need other arrangements which require a different level of evidence but still need an application to be made through AAO. These arrangements are: Alternative Accommodation (away from Centre), Bilingual Dictionary (with or without up to 25% extra time), Live Speaker, Practical Assistant, Sign Language Interpreter, Supervised Rest Breaks and Transcript[16].

Finally, there are a number of arrangements which no longer require prior approval but which can be allowed by the Centre if they are the candidate's normal way of working. No application through AAO is needed. These are:
- amplification equipment
- braillers
- closed circuit TV/OCR scanners
- colour naming for colour blind candidates
- coloured overlays
- low vision aids/magnifier
- prompter
- read aloud
- word processor

These arrangements will still have practical implications in terms of organisation and equipment, even though no permission is required.

---

[16] From September 2011 use of a transcript and use of a bilingual dictionary without extra time will be removed from AAO and become Centre-awarded arrangements.

> **Word Processors**
>
> Please note careful consideration must be given to JCQ interpretations of "normal way of working", especially in regard to **word processors**. It is not the JCQ intention that any student who requests a word processor should use one. You should be able to demonstrate that the word processor truly represents the candidate's normal practice in class and exams. Please see Chapter 8 for discussion.

- Students & parents should be informed of the outcome of online applications and decisions to grant other arrangements, and students will need practice in using their allocated access arrangement. For example having the help of a reader or scribe in class is a very different skill to using one under exam conditions.

LATE OCTOBER / EARLY NOVEMBER
- **or leading up to the examination period**

The SENCO needs to collaborate with the Exams Officer in arranging resources / personnel / accommodation for each examination or controlled assessment.

Staff acting as Readers, Scribes etc. will need training to ensure that they understand the requirements of their role.

DURING AND AFTER EACH EXAM SERIES

- Keep careful records of access arrangements used.
- Collect feedback sheets on effectiveness of access arrangements. (See example feedback form Chapter 6)

Guidelines for Staff, Information for Candidates and Parents

All staff have a role to play in identifying candidates who may need access arrangements. Therefore it is useful to circulate guidance throughout your Centre. Candidates and their parents also need up-to-date information. The following pages can be used as handouts for this purpose.

Guidelines for Subject Teachers, Tutors and Learning Support Staff

> Access arrangements allow candidates/learners to show what they know and can do without changing the demands of the assessment. (Joint Council for Qualifications 2010)

You are likely to be aware of candidates in your classes / teaching groups who have difficulties that may make them eligible for *access arrangements* in tests and public examinations. Please watch out for such candidates each year (especially if they are new to the school/college) and keep the SEN / ALS Department informed of their needs. It is likely that some kind of screening procedure will be carried out to identify these candidates, but there are always some who will not be identified through screening tests. The Learning Support staff are dependent on you to keep them informed of potential candidates for access arrangements.

It is essential that candidates are identified as early as possible in their school/college career for the following reasons:

The arrangements should be made at the start of the course wherever possible so that candidates know what is available and have the arrangements in place for module tests, course work and terminal papers. It is the Centre's responsibility to ensure that the regulations about who may act as '**Scribe**' for a candidate are not infringed during completion of course work.

The arrangements should reflect what help has to be given in the classroom and the normal way of working should reflect what is going to be available in the examinations.

Applications for permission to grant access arrangements must be made online early in the examination course, ideally at the start of Year 10 for GCSE in secondary schools, or on entry to FE College. There are deadlines for applications, and it may not be possible to process late applications within the few weeks before the examination.

Centres are required to have made sure that candidates have practised using their access arrangements in class tests, annual exams, and mock examinations. As a subject teacher you have some responsibility to make sure these opportunities are available.

The awarding bodies also require that candidates are entered for the correct level of examination. Broadly speaking, a candidate working below level 4 of the National Curriculum should not be entered for GCSE. An Entry Level qualification is likely to be more appropriate.

The main types of access arrangements available are as follows:

* **Extra Time**, for candidates who work very slowly
* **Rest Breaks**, for poor concentration or extreme stress
* Use of a **Bilingual Dictionary**, for candidates whose first language is not English, Irish or Welsh, subject to the regulations

- **Readers**, for **very** poor readers with decoding or comprehension difficulties who cannot read by themselves
- **Reading Aloud**, for those who have reading difficulties and can concentrate better if they can hear themselves read
- **Scribes**, for **very** poor or slow writers who cannot **write** by themselves
- **Word Processors**, for candidates who **use a WP in class**
- **Transcripts** of scripts which may be hard for the examiner to read
- **Prompters**, for candidates who lose concentration easily
- **Oral Language Modifiers,** for candidates who have problems with comprehension

(N.B. Your SENCO / ALS Manager will be able to advise you about more technical arrangements which may be required, e.g. for **candidates with a visual or hearing impairment or physical disability**.)

You may also be aware of candidates who rarely complete tests and exams in the time allowed, but who may be missed by brief screening tests. Please keep your SENCO / ALS Manager informed of these candidates.

Please note that there is no specific access arrangement for poor spelling, unless it is **so** poor that it is likely to impair the examiner's ability to read the candidate's answers. In this case a Transcript, or in extreme cases, a Scribe may be appropriate. If spellings are reasonable phonic approximations, and so can be deciphered, no access arrangements can be offered.

Regulations have changed in the last few years, and a diagnosis of dyslexia is no longer sufficient to allow a candidate extra time. The awarding bodies now require *'evidence of need in the normal working arrangements'*, i.e. the candidate uses extra time in class and for tests and internal exams.

Summary

Although the processes of screening, applying for and implementing access arrangements are the responsibility of the SENCO / ALS Manager and Exams Officer, all teaching and support staff have a central role to play in the identification of candidates who need adjustments during public examinations and training the students to use agreed access arrangements effectively.

Read, C (2011) The SENCO's Year in Jones, A (Ed) **Dyslexia: Assessing the need for access arrangements during examinations**, 4th edition. Patoss, Evesham (Available from www.patoss-dyslexia.org.uk) These guidelines may be photocopied for use in your Centre. They refer to Access Arrangements, Reasonable Adjustments and Special Consideration. 1 September 2010 – 31 August 2011. (www.jcq.org.uk)

Access Arrangements - Introductory Information for Candidates

Access Arrangements are 'reasonable adjustments' for you if you have a disability, a temporary injury or a special educational need that significantly affects you in exams.

Access arrangements might mean you have support from a member of staff in the exam or a small change might be made – for example the time allowed. Access arrangements

- do *not* **change** the skills or knowledge being tested
- *must not* **give an unfair advantage**, *but ..*
- **do give a level playing field** so you can show your skills and knowledge.

There is a "menu" of arrangements on offer - the most commonly used are:

- **Extra Time** - for candidates who read or write slowly
- **Rest Breaks** - a short break from the exam to help those with very poor concentration, extreme stress or who might need a break for medical reasons
- **Reading Aloud** - for those who work more effectively if they hear themselves read
- **Word Processors** - for candidates who always use a word processor in class and exams – the word processor will have to be specially set up for the exams.
- **Transcripts** – if your handwriting is quite difficult for the examiner to read, your teachers will use your exact words but write them out again so they are easier to read.
- **Bilingual Dictionary** - for those who have English as an Additional Language
- **Readers** - for those who need help with reading
- **Scribes** - for those who have writing difficulties – perhaps you write very slowly, or your spelling or grammar is very weak, or your handwriting is illegible.
- **Prompters** – for those who lose concentration very easily
- **Oral Language Modifiers -** for those who have problems with comprehension and a supporter is needed to re-phrase the questions, but not the technical language.

You may be able to have one or more of these access arrangements in an exam if that is your normal way of working in your class or on your course. Which arrangement you have will also depend on **your needs** AND the **type of exam** AND the **current regulations**. This means different arrangements might be allowed in different exams.

Supporters in an Exam

If you need someone to give you support in an exam – such as a reader, a scribe or a prompter – remember they cannot be a relative or a friend and they cannot:

- explain or discuss the question
- help with your answer or comment on your work
- tell you when to move on to the next question.

The rules around access arrangements are strict, and if you or a member of staff are found to be breaking them you may lose marks in your assessments. **If you have any questions about access arrangements speak to your teacher.**

From: ***Dyslexia: Assessing the Need for Access Arrangements during Examinations***, 4th edition. Patoss, Evesham (www.patoss-dyslexia.org.uk) These notes may be photocopied for use in your Centre. They refer to JCQ regulations 1 September 2010 – 31 August 2011. (www.jcq.org.uk)

Access Arrangements - Introductory Information for Parents

Access Arrangements are 'reasonable adjustments' for students who have a disability, a temporary injury or a special educational need **that significantly affects them in exams**.

Assessments to Establish Access Arrangements

A specialist assessment may be needed to support an access arrangement application. We will co-ordinate this if it is needed and use it to help make decisions about exams. Please do speak to school senior staff before arranging any assessment yourself as the school is not obliged to automatically accept the findings of a privately commissioned report. No-one is guaranteed an arrangement simply because they have a learning difficulty – evidence is needed to show the impact it has on the student in school.

We will always seek to work with parents to ensure the most appropriate outcome for students. Please speak to your son / daughter's teacher or the school Special Educational Needs Co-ordinator if you have concerns and we will be happy to advise.

Access arrangements

- **do *not* change** the skills or knowledge being tested,
- ***must not* give an unfair advantage**, *but ..*
- **do give a level playing field** so students can show their knowledge.

There is a "menu" of arrangements on offer. Students may be able to have one or more of these. The precise arrangement depends on: the **student's needs** AND their **normal way of working** in class AND the **type of exam** AND the **current regulations**. This means different arrangements might be allowed in different exams but all arrangements should reflect normal practice so last minute applications are rarely permitted.

The most commonly used arrangements are:

- **Extra Time** - for candidates who read or write slowly
- **Rest Breaks** - a short break from the exam to help those with very poor concentration, extreme stress or who might need a break for medical reasons
- **Reading Aloud** - for those who work more effectively if they hear themselves read
- **Word Processors** - for candidates who use a word processor in class and exams – the word processor will have to be specially set up for the exams.
- **Transcripts** – for those whose handwriting is difficult for the examiner to read.
- **Bilingual Dictionary** - for those who have English as an Additional Language
- **Readers** - for those who need help with reading
- **Scribes** - for those who have writing difficulties – those who write very slowly, whose spelling or grammar is very weak, or whose handwriting is illegible.
- **Prompters** – for those who lose concentration very easily
- **Oral Language Modifiers** - for those who have problems with comprehension and a supporter is needed to re-phrase the exam questions, but not the technical language.

*From: **Dyslexia: Assessing the Need for Access Arrangements during Examinations**, 4th edition. Patoss, Evesham (www.patoss-dyslexia.org.uk) These notes may be photocopied for use in your Centre. They refer to JCQ regulations 1 September 2010 – 31 August 2011. (www.jcq.org.uk)

8. Notes for Specialist Teachers

This chapter discusses in detail the role of the Specialist Teacher in access arrangements. While the Head of Centre is ultimately responsible for all access arrangements, the Specialist Teacher clearly shares a professional duty to support the fairness of the system. The JCQ define this as ensuring that:

- the rigour of testing of candidates is maintained
- the quality of reports is such that all required evidence is provided to justify requests
- arrangements are recommended only for those with genuine and formally identified needs which reflect their normal way of working within the Centre.

To meet these goals, the JCQ require Heads of Centres to take responsibility for the quality of the access arrangements process, including the appointment of assessors whose qualifications and experience are fit for purpose.

Specialist Teacher Training and Qualifications

To undertake access arrangements assessments the Head of Centre needs to be satisfied that you, the Specialist Teacher, are "suitably qualified" for the job. Although, the JCQ no longer approve individual qualifications they do give recommendations for appropriate skills and knowledge for assessors of candidates with learning difficulties. They are that the assessor should be:

- able to **teach** and **assess** secondary age/adult students who have learning difficulties
- knowledgeable regarding both the theory and practice of assessment of learning difficulties – underlying ability, all aspects of literacy, as well as diagnostic tests.
- able to select appropriate assessment materials in an informed way and have the ability to interpret results correctly.
- trained and experienced in cognitive ability testing and able to judge when referral to another professional is needed.

In addition assessors must have:
- thorough understanding of the JCQ regulations
- familiarity with the Equality Act (2010) and how it applies to qualifications.

As the JCQ require conclusions and recommendations to be based on the results of standardised tests, it is imperative that Specialist Teachers fully understand the principles of psychometric testing and how it is used to support their professional opinions. (For a summary see Chapter 9, *Basic Concepts in Psychometrics.*)

Therefore, to meet JCQ recommendations, a "suitably qualified" Specialist Teacher is likely to have successfully completed a lengthy, in-depth course focusing on teaching and assessing learners with SpLDs in the relevant age range, where their competence in carrying out full diagnostic assessments was directly observed.

If you completed your SpLD qualification several years ago you should update your skills with training geared to the assessment role. The SpLD Assessment Standards Committee[17] (SASC) has recently launched an authorised provider scheme to assure the quality of assessment continuing professional development. The SASC website aims to list training events from across the wide spectrum of educational institutions and SpLD organisations.

SpLD Assessment Practising Certificate (APC)

The SpLD APC came into being following the DfES 2005 / SpLD Working Party, whose work initially investigated SpLD assessment needs in Higher Education. However, its final report and the APC scheme has recently been endorsed as a useful quality standard for schools by the Rose Review (2009) – *Identifying and Teaching Children and Young People with Dyslexia and Literacy Difficulties.*[18]

As an overarching professional practice certificate the APC recognises that the holder has the relevant knowledge and competence in assessment of SpLDs, is committed to continuing development of their skills and follows a professional code of ethics – all needed for those conducting assessments for access arrangements.

Patoss and Dyslexia Action currently issue the APC; the BDA will also soon be offering this service. To gain and renew the certificate practitioners must demonstrate skills in full diagnostic assessment, including investigation of literacy skills, general underlying ability and cognitive processing skill using up-to-date resources. While the everyday practice of providing evidence for access arrangements does not always call for this depth of assessment, given that a diagnosis of SpLD is not required, assessors are best placed to make good decisions if they have this breadth and depth of knowledge.

Therefore, Patoss recommends that a Head of Centre regard the following as the order of priority in looking for "appropriate" Specialist Teacher qualifications:

1.   a current SpLD Assessment Practising Certificate **OR**
2.   a qualification accredited by the BDA as meeting AMBDA requirements[19] **OR**
3.   a qualification listed on the JCQ website **OR**
4.   in the case of assessments for students who are hearing impaired or have moderate learning difficulties, Heads of Centres may wish to consider other qualifications.

---

[17] SASC is supported by the DfE, DBIS, Patoss, BDA, BPS, Dyslexia Action, HADC and numerous training providers

[18] DCSF (2009) *Identifying and Teaching Children and Young People with Dyslexia and Literacy Difficulties (Rose Review)* DCSF: London.

[19] Please note it is not a requirement that professionals are 'active' Associate Members of the British Dyslexia Association (BDA) – simply that their qualification met the guidelines for Associate Membership of the BDA (AMBDA) at the time it was completed.

We must point out that the JCQ does not require assessors to hold an Assessment Practising Certificate. However, it is widely considered a model of good practice for Specialist Teachers assessing students with SpLD.

The JCQ prefer that a Specialist Teacher employed within the Centre carries out assessments. Specialist Teachers employed at other Centres or by the Local Authority are an option, as are independent practitioners who work closely with a school or college. Thus, few outside agencies should be involved in the process, especially those who employ people who are neither teachers nor psychologists.

The Specialist Teacher can only carry out the assessment by working closely with the Centre, which will manage the process for each candidate. Your own working context will clearly make a big difference here; if you work in the Centre the collaboration needed will be that much easier.

It is particularly important for all independent practitioners to uphold this principle of collaboration between themselves, the Centre and the staff who teach any students that they agree to assess. You may place SENCOs in a difficult position or even in dispute with parents, over expectations that arrangements will be allowed in a Centre at the behest of an independent practitioner (whether Psychologist or Specialist Teacher). Therefore, independent practitioners are advised to:

- discuss the matter with the SENCO beforehand and/or
- make it quite clear to the candidate that the decision regarding access arrangements can only be made by the Centre.

If you regularly assesses for a number of Centres you should ensure that each one has a note of your specialist SpLD qualifications, and a copy of your certificate, and that they notify the JCQ that you are a Specialist Teacher contracted to work for them, either using AAO or Form 8A depending on the qualifications for which you assess. Note the focus is on the Centre to see that those assessing for them are notified to the JCQ, either through the online or paper-based system.

> Do make sure the Centre registers your name and qualifications with the JCQ so your reports can be accepted as evidence.

Insurance

Specialist Teachers (as well as Psychologists) have a duty of care to learners with regard to the advice that they give. Therefore, they should ensure they are fully covered in the role of assessor in this context. If you are self-employed, adequate insurance is clearly essential. If employed you are advised not only to check that your employer covers you, but also to remind them that they are vicariously liable for any errors/omissions etc. that their employees may be held to have perpetrated. Insurance should be in place for both legal expenses and any damages awarded to provide cover should any action be brought against you for failure to make a proper diagnosis, appropriate recommendations, etc.

Professional Indemnity insurance is available through Patoss to its members. This is the only group insurance policy available to SpLD Specialist Teachers/assessors in this role.

Self-employed professionals should make sure they know about the requirements of the Data Protection Act and its current regulations[20].

The Assessment

There are a number of variables to do with when and how a candidate is referred for a Specialist Teacher assessment, which have implications for what we do and say.

The appointment might be at any time during the learner's secondary education or whilst he is in the FE sector. Perhaps it is the first time he has ever been assessed, or he may have had one or more assessments previously. The request may have been triggered primarily because of impending exams – or only partly. All of this will become clear through the background information you collect when planning the assessment session.

If you work in the candidate's Centre or Local Authority you are likely to be carrying out the assessment because his teachers think it necessary or his parents have pressed for an assessment. Older candidates, especially in FE, may self-refer.

Determining the precise needs of the assessment will need a little more research if you are working outside the Centre. As an independent practitioner you might be asked to work in a Centre which has no qualified Specialist Teacher on staff. Other common situations are that a private assessment is recommended because staff do not have the time to do one themselves, are not sure whether, or do not agree that access arrangements are necessary. In all circumstances – but particularly the last two cited – sound professional practice and courtesy require that you make contact with the Centre **before** carrying out the assessment.

For all assessors, it is imperative that you inform the candidate (and parents) that you are not the sole arbiter in the decision regarding access arrangements. Centre staff will use the information you provide, in conjunction with their knowledge of the student's normal way of working, to make decisions about his need for adjustments under the prevailing regulations (which may have changed since the date of the assessment).

As you get to know the circumstances and needs of your learner you can carefully choose the assessment materials you will need and the approach you will take. From here on, we will consider the situation when the referral is primarily to do with exams.

Before you begin assessments make certain you are familiar with the current regulations each year and the "menu" of access arrangements which are available.

---

[20]For further information see www.ico.gov.uk or
www.justice.gov.uk/guidance/docs/how_data_protection_affects_my_business.pdf

Competence in assessment for SpLDs – both theory and practice – is assumed. For teachers wishing to refresh their knowledge in this regard, the joint Patoss / Hodder Murray publication edited by Backhouse and Morris (2005)[21] is a useful reference.

Assessment Materials

Theoretically, you will not know which access arrangement, if any, might be justified at the beginning of an assessment, so you should have a range of materials available. You must use **up-to-date, age-appropriate, nationally standardised tests**, where such a test is published. Assessment resources continue to be developed and new editions made available so there is every opportunity to use appropriate tests; you should avoid tests which hardly, or do not, cover the age of the candidate. You should make sure you check test catalogues each year in order to maintain best practice regarding your assessment materials.

Tests which can be administered to a group are clearly useful and will save time if you work within a Centre. However, for you to include group test information in your specialist report, you must have conducted the test yourself, rather than delegated this task to other staff.

> NB. Screening resources are not suitable for use as core evidence in access arrangements applications. That is not to say they do not have many uses for the Specialist Teacher, just that their results should not be relied upon for evidence in this context. Please see notes on screening materials at the end of this chapter.

Do take care to study the standardised test administration instructions and follow them carefully in your assessment session to ensure the reliability of your result.

Overall, we should not forget the dictum "*tests don't diagnose, people do*". Whilst severe difficulties may be obvious, differentiating the genuine but less severe cases from the wide range of "average" students takes specialist experience. Standardised testing supplemented by careful questioning and observation are all part of a sound assessment and will reveal which aspects of language and literacy are effortful and stress inducing for a learner, and are especially helpful to the Centre in making decisions about access arrangements.

Evaluating a Test

While the following pages outline the main tests useful for access arrangements, the list is not exhaustive and new tests are being published all the time. Also, as the JCQ does not publish a list of acceptable tests, you have to evaluate tests to see if they match the needs of your students. A useful approach might be to check the test against the questions in Figure 8.1 below. However, keep in mind that tests are rarely perfect so you must balance their strengths and weaknesses to make a judgement.

---

[21] Backhouse, G and Morris, K (2005) *Dyslexia? Assessing and Reporting, the Patoss Guide* Hodder Murray: London

Figure 8.1   Evaluating a Test

Is the test "a good fit" with my students?	
• When was it published? Do I have the most up-to-date edition?	It is important to compare candidates against the most up-to-date information available, to give a fair representation of the population now. It is recommended that tests are less than 10 years old, although this presents a significant problem at present for some key areas of testing!
• What age range does it cover?	The test should more than span the age of the candidate, as results at the very edges of test ranges are less reliable.
• Has it been standardised using a large and diverse sample population?	A better and bigger sample will more likely include similar individuals to the candidate and thus give a fairer comparison. *See Chapter 9.*
• Where was it developed?	A UK test will be preferable if one is available but USA tests are fully acceptable.

Is the test "a good fit" with the assessment needs?	
• Does the test measure what it claims to measure? Is it valid?	A valid test ensures the test activities are good tools to measure the target skills. *See Chapter 9 for discussion of test validity.*
• Does the manual give standard scores?	Standard scores based on a mean of 100 are most often, though not always, required by AAO so these are most useful. Other types of score can be converted.
• Is it an individual and/or group test?	Group tests can help with the workload but do not allow close investigation of individual strengths and weaknesses.
• Are parallel forms available?	These allow you to compare progress over a short period of time. Tests without parallel forms often require *at least* 6 months before you can re-use them.

Is the test statistically sound?	
• Does the manual include information about test reliability? Does it give consistent results?	A reliable test does what is says on the tin: gives a reliable, replicable result. *See Chapter 9 for detail on reliability statistics.*
• Will the format of the test work for my students?	A good test needs to be accessible in terms of print, layout, paper quality and the provision of practice items. If online, do layouts or IT skill requirements influence the result?
• Will this test fit into my work environment? What are the ongoing costs?	The best test in the world is no good if it takes so long to administer, mark and score you could never fit it into your working day!

The Access Arrangement Report

The standards and type of evidence to be presented in an assessment report should clearly be the same in all cases across the country in the interests of fairness. Specialist Teachers conducting the assessment and the Centre must be scrupulous in the standards they apply. They must be comfortable that these would stand up under an investigation. Therefore, it is essential that supporting evidence is both obtained and retained for every access arrangement application.

It is also extremely helpful to JCQ Centre Inspectors if this evidence is presented in a similar way. As Inspectors are not trained in diagnostic assessment themselves, they can then see at a glance whether a proper assessment has been carried out. Your Exams Officer will also be pleased if the Specialist Teacher report supplies the precise information needed to make applications in an easily accessible way. Therefore, it is strongly recommended that you use a consistent record sheet to summarise your findings for each candidate. Some samples of Specialist Teacher record forms are provided at the end of this chapter.

Figure 8.2: What's In a Name? What makes a "diagnostic assessment report?"

Specialist Teachers carry out assessments to establish the learning difficulties faced by a student. As there is potential for confusion around the term "diagnostic assessment" and "learning difficulties" in this context, some clarification might be useful as it has an impact on professional practice.

A "full diagnostic assessment" investigates the cognitive and attainment profile of an individual in order to diagnose an SpLD, and gives recommendations for the learner. This type of assessment is required to support an application for the Disabled Students Allowances in Higher Education. Thus, Patoss recommends that wherever possible a full assessment meeting the DfES 2005 / SpLD Working Party Guidelines is undertaken for a 16+ student who plans to go to HE. This way the student can avoid further assessment and use the report to provide evidence of his disability. If this is not possible, you should make sure he understands that further assessment will be necessary.

A "diagnostic assessment" in the context of access arrangements is more limited as it does not require the confirmation of a Specific Learning Difficulty – just that a difficulty in learning exists, specifically a difficulty that affects performance in examinations and assessments. These two understandings of "diagnostic assessment" are quite different things. In the case of access arrangements the professional selects only those tests they feel are necessary to show the difficulties experienced by the candidate. When collated this specialist test information is referred to by the JCQ as the diagnostic report – and they suggest it is recorded in Section C of Form 8 or a Centre-devised equivalent. Professionals should make students and/or parents aware that this is unlikely to constitute a diagnosis of an SpLD, depending on the depth of the assessment made.

Form 8 – Application for Access Arrangements: the Profile of Learning Difficulties

In the recent past, all access arrangements applications had to be made using JCQ Form 8[22]. With the advent of AAO the imperative for the form has been removed, for GCSE/GCE applications, but the need for a way to record the evidence has not. Therefore, the JCQ recommends that the evidence still be collated on **Form 8,** or alternatively **a Centre-devised equivalent**, **which addresses the same key questions** and allows the specialist to sign to confirm they conducted the assessment.

To help our discussion of the evidence requirements we will assume that Form 8 will be retained, which is the practice in many Centres. A copy of the form is on the JCQ website.

From the JCQ perspective, specialists who do formal assessments are not required to make direct recommendations about "appropriate entry" or "special arrangements" but to contribute evidence of learning difficulties. This takes professional skill and judgement, particularly in less obvious cases.

In the role of "Qualified Specialist" you therefore need only supply diagnostic information and sign to confirm you have conducted the assessment. This is recorded in section C of Form 8. Sections A and B are completed by the Centre - section A before the assessment, section B after it. Section A summarises the background information about the candidate: his needs, his normal way of working and the additional provision he has received to date. In the case of a late diagnosis, or where no history exits, this might mean your Centres' screening results and current support arrangements. The Centre completes section B after the assessment, when your recommendations alongside evidence of need are considered together to decide on the right arrangement. Of course, it is entirely likely that the same person completes all sections if they have multiple roles within the Centre!

Section C - Form 8 ...

also known as "the diagnostic report" (See Figure 8.2, page 73 above)

Whatever other purposes have informed your assessment plan (e.g. teaching recommendations), remember that *here you are only required* to report on those aspects of the candidate's difficulties which will help the Centre decide whether an access arrangement might [a] be justified and [b] mitigate the effects of his problem. However, you may have to, and indeed want to, explore wider aspects of the student's profile so you can give him, his teachers and the Centre the most useful information to decide between arrangements and to support teaching. **After all, the access arrangement should only be one part of the school or college's support for the student and as a Specialist Teacher you are in an excellent position to suggest good ways forward.**

---

[22] This form can be downloaded from www.jcq.org.uk – look under Exams Office / Forms

Standardised scores (SS), with a mean of 100, should be reported wherever possible. Since the *descriptions* allocated to various ranges of scores (e.g. average, low average, etc.) vary from one test manual to another, the JCQ have ruled that:

- the only test results which can be described as "**below average**" are those which are more than 1 standard deviation (SD) below the mean (i.e. SS of 84 or less).

In addition, from September 2011 additional clarification in description of scores will be provided such that:

- the only test results which can be described as "**low average**" are those below 90 and above 84 (ie SS of 85 – 89)

In the interests of supporting a fair, nationwide system, it is strongly recommended that this is applied to all standardised tests, whether reading, writing or cognitive.

Section C gives the opportunity to report skills under three headings:
- **reading skills** – including accuracy, speed and comprehension
- **writing skills** – including accuracy, legibility, speed and quality of language
- **other relevant information** – the home for information that cannot be included elsewhere which paints a picture of the candidate. Relevant and concise case history notes might be included here and/ or the results of other attainment or cognitive tests, e.g. verbal and non-verbal ability, verbal memory, phonological processing, perceptual-motor skills, non-word reading fluency etc.

The rest of this chapter is split into the above three headings, with appropriate tests listed under the section where they would be reported in evidence. Also see Chapter 12 where all tests are listed for ease of comparison.

Reading Skills

A primary consideration is whether the candidate is likely to be able to read the examination paper accurately, with understanding and within a normal time frame.

The JCQ regulations concerning provision of reading assistance acknowledge that reading is a complex skill and that there are various aspects with which candidates can have difficulties.
- Candidates whose single word reading **accuracy** impairs their understanding
- Candidates who read so **slowly** that they lose the sense of the text – even when given extra time to re-read
- Candidates with **poor comprehension** of language may who may need to hear text read rather than having to decode and try to understand simultaneously, or who would benefit from an oral language modifier or modified paper.

Reading skills may need to be assessed in a variety of ways – at word & text level, timed and untimed – before a true picture of a candidate's skills and potential needs for access arrangements can be assessed. It is probably true to say that where reading ability is already known to be extremely limited, a graded single word test will suffice as evidence of need for a reader. Where the difficulties are less obvious, a more thorough examination will be required.

More than one strategy can be used to access text. Good use of one can mask weaknesses in another; for example, whole word recognition and "reading for meaning" can supplement and compensate for weak decoding. The latter, however, may make the candidate prone to errors in stressful situations where accurate reading is vital, as is the case in reading exam questions!

Perhaps the most valid type of test to use when evaluating the need for reading assistance is one which requires the candidate to read continuous text silently and respond to comprehension questions, under timed conditions. This mirrors the exam situation most closely. These timed comprehension tests are particularly relevant in this context since results will assist the Centre in decisions regarding the need for extra time.

A selection of reading tests should therefore be available which focus on accuracy, speed and comprehension and are suitable for different types of candidate.

Reading Accuracy

Form 8: Section C
Question 1

An **untimed** graded single word test which supplies a standardised score should be used here. (Tests are listed alphabetically.)

> The tests below could be used to support an application for a **reader / computer reader**

- **Hodder Oral Reading Tests (HORT) (5 – 16+ years)**
An individual test which is quick to administer with an accessible manual, the HORT includes three complementary tests – **graded single word reading**, plus sentence reading and reading speed. There are two parallel forms.

- **Single Word Reading Test (6 – 16 years)**
Another quick-to-administer word reading test designed for checking progress at regular intervals. It contains six graded sets of ten words of increasing difficulty. For individual administration it provides diagnostic information and includes parallel forms.

- **Wechsler Individual Achievement Test – 2nd UK edition for Teachers (WIAT-II-UK-T) (4 – 85:11 years)**
The graded word reading test in this battery incorporates assessment of letter identification, phonological awareness, letter-sound awareness and decoding skills for use with younger pupils. The test is un-timed, but a mechanism for assessing "automaticity" of word reading is included. **The UK norms go up to 16:11 years only**. USA norms can be used for older candidates. Reading comprehension, reading speed and spelling tests are included (see below).

- **Wide Range Achievement Test – 4th edition (WRAT-4) (5 – 94 years)**

The single word subtest measures letter and word reading. Assessors should be aware that the manual states 10 seconds are allowed for each word, but this is considered and accepted as an un-timed test. The WRAT4 is an American test, but distributed and widely used in the UK. It contains parallel forms - blue, green and a combined form. Standard scores are easily obtained from the manual. WRAT4 also provides a sentence comprehension test (see below) and an arithmetic test.

See also **Dyslexia Portfolio** (page 89)– this is a combined test including both literacy and processing skills.

Specialist Teachers working with Psychologists may also have access to the BAS & WORD reading tests, but cannot purchase these resources themselves.

Other types of reading test can be used to investigate word level reading skills. However, such supplementary evidence regarding the candidate's speed/fluency or decoding competence should be reported in the "Other Relevant Information" section and appropriate tests are listed in that section of this chapter.

Reading Comprehension and Speed

Form 8: Section C
Question 2

A candidate might be able to read accurately but his comprehension of what he reads, and the time it takes, can also mean he requires reading assistance.

The tests below can contribute to an application for a **reader/computer reader, extra time, or oral language modifier.** Not all tests will provide all the required evidence.

Tests of comprehension and reading speed should provide a standard score.

However, Patoss recognises that for some **older** candidates no tests are published which provide a reliable standardised measure of reading speed. Therefore, we advise the following options are considered.

For older candidates only where no standardised test of reading speed is published	**For award of a reader**: It is likely that the student whose reading speed is incredibly slow will also have below average scores on a reading accuracy or a timed comprehension test so these can be used instead of a direct speed measure to award the reader.
	For the award of extra time over 25%: Other well below average processing measures will have to be sought to provide the required evidence. These can be drawn from the cognitive processing tests listed in this chapter.

Reading speed can be given as a rate in words per minute (wpm) if a standard score is not available for awards of up to 25% extra time.

Oral Reading

Oral reading tests enable close observation and monitoring of skills and strategies. Therefore, they are especially appropriate when the assessment has a dual purpose: to establish entitlement to access arrangements and to plan an educational intervention. On the whole they only measure how quickly the passages are read **before** the comprehension questions are posed. Therefore, the speed measures – whilst entirely valid in themselves – may be less appropriate for the more able reader who, whilst fairly accurate, has to re-read before he has fully grasped the meaning or who reads aloud more slowly than he does silently. Specialist Teachers should carefully consider this dimension of reading assessment.

Oral Reading Tests

- **Adult Reading Test (ART) (16 – 25+ years)**

This test has been criticised on the grounds of the rather limited standardisation sample (comparatively small and restricted to 6 FE/HE institutions in and around London). It is quite lengthy to administer, and comprehension relies on recall, as there is no opportunity to revisit the text. Nearly a quarter of the standardisation sample were students with EAL. Since their data is provided as a separate set of norms, this resource may be of use in similar contexts. This test provides percentile measures of reading rate, comprehension and accuracy. They may be converted to standard scores using any other test manual. However, the score is often supplied as a range and so is less precise than might be preferred for access arrangements purposes.

- **Diagnostic Reading Analysis – 2ⁿᵈ edition (DRA) (7 – 16:05 years)**

The DRA, developed specifically for use with poor readers, contains both fiction and non-fiction passages, graded for each age-level, which closely match the National Literacy Strategy (NLS). The test has 2 parallel forms for retesting. It incorporates a passage for assessing whether listening comprehension is age appropriate and the pupil's performance on this part determines the level at which he should start the reading assessment. The test is designed so that pupils need only read three passages as a rule and should take no more than 15 minutes altogether, thus making it more efficient than some others. A standard score for text-level reading accuracy is derived and measures of fluency/reading rate, comprehension and comprehension processing speed can be obtained and converted into one of five descriptive categories which in turn relate to a band of standardised scores.

- **Gray Oral Reading Tests - 4th edition (GORT 4) (6 – 18:11 years)**

An oral reading fluency score (i.e. not taking time needed for comprehension into account) is derived from separate rate & accuracy results in this American test, which has 2 parallel forms. Words are supplied if a candidate cannot read them in the comprehension test and so this score does not necessarily represent the student's ability to understand text without help. Some of the content and ways in which words are used may be unfamiliar to UK candidates and so this test may not always be suitable in this context – most especially for candidates of low ability, or whose first language is not English.

- **Wechsler Individual Achievement Test - 2nd UK edition for teachers (WIAT-II-UK-T) (4 – 85:11 years)**

This is a thorough test of sentence and text level comprehension, which also gives a standard score for reading speed. Overlapping sets of age-specific items are provided. If the set proves too difficult, the previous one must be administered. The candidate can choose to read the passages **aloud or silently** and is timed as doing so - but the sentences must be read aloud. Comprehension questions are posed after each item. **Reading speed norms are only available up to 16:11.** (WIAT also tests reading accuracy and spelling)

- **Wide Range Achievement Test – Expanded (WRAT-E) Individual Assessment Form I (5 – 24:11 years)**

This test is often used with higher ability/attainment native English speaking students. Some of the passages reflect the American context but it has age-graded levels of difficulty and lower levels can be administered if needed, although no words can be read for the candidate. No standardised reading speed score is provided, but wpm could be informally calculated. It includes additional testing materials in mathematics and a group testing version is available, see below.

- **York Assessment of Reading for Comprehension – Passage Reading Secondary (11-16 years)**

In this new individual test the candidate may read silently or aloud, without affecting the standardisation, and the time taken recorded. He may refer back to the text if necessary to answer the comprehension questions but not when giving the summary which is requested at the end of the test. Standard scores are derived for reading rate, fluency and comprehension and parallel forms are available. Supplementary passages are also provided for students with greater decoding difficulties; these require reading aloud and give a further score for accuracy.

Silent Reading

As suggested above, **timed** silent reading tests are arguably more useful for this context. Most, but not all, of the tests listed below meet this need.

In all the tests here, responses to comprehension questions are by multiple choice and so no extended writing is involved. When considering access arrangements, provide the candidate with a different colour pen to record his answers (or even 2 different colours!!) and allow him to continue with the test for another 25% (or 10%, then the full 25%). In this way you can judge whether a poor score is essentially to do with speed or whether he still cannot cope with aspects of the assessment no matter how much extra time is given.

Silent Reading Tests

- **Access Reading Test (7 – 20+ years)**

This test gives useful diagnostic information regarding a candidate's skills in four key areas – literal comprehension; vocabulary; understanding requiring inference or prediction;

comprehension requiring analysis, as well as an overall score. There are two parallel forms & administration takes a maximum of 30 minutes (plus extra time if considered appropriate).

- **Edinburgh Reading Test 4 (ERT4) (11 – 16 years)**

A total score plus a diagnostic profile is generated from the candidate's performance on the different sections of the test. This gives valuable comparative information about his reading strategies and ability to skim for information, read carefully for facts, perceive the consistency of various points of view in text, use inference and understand word meanings, useful for remedial work as well as considering appropriate access arrangements. Section B (Vocabulary) is often a particular challenge for dyslexic candidates whose single word reading and oral vocabulary are not well developed – an entirely different situation from simply running out of time. Standard administration time is 45 minutes; testing may be continued for an extra 11¼ minutes to gauge attainment given extra time. A combined Scorer / Profiler CD-Rom (Version 2) provides computerised diagnostic profiling.

- **Edinburgh Reading Test 4 – Interactive (ERT4i) (11:7 years – adult)**

This is a version of the ERT4 which the student takes on screen. The tests are **as above** and the programme then calculates scores attained during the standard 45 minute test time and again including 25% extra time.

- **Gray Silent Reading Tests (GSRT) (7 – 25 years)**

Although this test has a higher "ceiling" than the others mentioned here, as well as 2 parallel forms, it has the disadvantage of not having a time limit which is particularly pertinent in this context. However, more able students can do very well on this test because it is untimed and the passage can be referred back to as often as necessary. Results could be compared with attainment under timed conditions to give qualitative evidence of improved performance when given sufficient time. However, it is important to note that if the student makes more than the permitted number of errors on the initial passage it is necessary to go back to the previous level, and so on, until the required basal is met. This means that is necessary to mark the test at the time of assessment.

- **Hodder Group Reading Tests: New Edition (HGRT) (5 – 16+ years)**

Test 3 in this group is suitable for ages 9:05 – 16+. Comprehension is assessed at word, sentence and text level using sentence completion and cloze techniques. 30 minutes are allowed for completion of the test at secondary level, and students can be given an additional 7½ minutes (25% extra), using a different colour pen to see if their performance improves significantly given more time. However, most pupils are expected to finish the test easily within the half hour.

- **Wide Range Achievement Test – Expanded (WRAT-E) Group Assessment Form G (7 – 18:11 years)**

This is suitable for use with older, higher ability candidates, but you should consider whether the occasional American spellings (e.g. characterize, tumor) and inclusion of American place names (e.g. Pennsylvania, Connecticut) are likely to affect comprehension. The test can be used to explore performance with and without extra time. This resource also contains non-verbal reasoning and maths tests. An individual form is available - see oral reading tests above.

- **Wide Range Achievement Test – 4th edition (WRAT- 4) (5 – 94 years)**

The WRAT-4 offers only a sentence-level comprehension subtest – rather than continuous text – so this may be a limitation in some contexts, although useful for weaker readers for whom continuous text is very difficult. Also, as it is un-timed other tests may be needed to provide supplementary information in regard to speed.

- **York Assessment of Reading for Comprehension – Passage Reading Secondary (11-16 years)**

See description above under Oral Reading Tests

Writing Skills

Where reading accuracy and comprehension scores should be reported as standardised scores for access arrangement purposes, the same hard and fast rule is acknowledged to be less straightforward with regard to **writing attainments**, since there are many qualitative aspects to these skills. However, assessors should endeavour to adhere to the same standards.

- Standardised scores for **spelling** are widely available and should be reported.
- A standardised score for **writing speed** is recommended where age appropriate test materials are published but a "words per minute" measure is also acceptable evidence for some arrangements.
- More tricky than the spelling and writing speed issues are the qualitative decisions which must be taken as to legibility and content.

There are several issues here.
- Is it likely that the examiner will be unable to decipher what this candidate writes, given his spelling and handwriting?
- Is his writing "incomprehensible" due to weak grammar and syntax?
- Is this candidate unable to demonstrate his knowledge and skills within time constraints given his writing competence and speed?
- Does his written output improve significantly if he uses a word processor or has more time? Or does he prefer to hand-write?
- If he is not competent with a word processor, is there a real difference in the quality/quantity of his output if he dictates to someone else?

Given the range of questions **writing will likely need to be assessed in relation to both spelling and free writing skills.**

Accuracy and Legibility
Spelling

Spelling should be assessed at word and text level. Initially you are only asked to comment on word-level spelling; a standardised score should be recorded. Tests below are suitable.

A low spelling score might be because of **_minor errors,_** but it could also be because of **_bizarre spellings_** and/or **atrocious handwriting** which make it extremely difficult to guess what each word might have been. The latter types are of particular interest in this context, as it is helpful to note the "percentage of errors **_unrecognisable_** as target word". Calculate this percentage out of the total number of words **attempted.**

> These tests could contribute to evidence for a **scribe or a word processor with spell check enabled.**

- **Diagnostic Spelling Tests 3 – 5 (Hodder) (9 – 25+ years)**

Three different tests are supplied in one pack, covering age groups 9-12, 11-15, 15-20+ years. Two parallel forms are provided as photocopiable masters for tests 4 & 5. Each word is dictated in a sentence and students are allowed 15 seconds to respond, so exceptionally slow spelling fluency can be noted. Each test takes about 15 minutes to administer. Standardised scores are derived. The words in test 3 are taken from the National Literacy Strategy; three quarters of the words in test 4 are taken from Key Stage 3 vocabulary lists of the major school subjects. Test 5 contains words most commonly mis-spelled by adults and focuses on functional literacy. The concise and easy-to-use manual includes diagnostic information and follow-up activities.

- **Helen Arkell Spelling Test (HAST) (5 – 17+ years)**

This test is designed to be diagnostic but also gives standardised scores. The test items represent the normal development of spelling and range from high to low frequency words. The assessor can describe the candidate's spelling profile and recommend a starting point for remediation.

- **Vernon Graded Word Spelling Test - 3rd edition (5 – 18+ years)**

This well-known test has now been completely revised and re-standardised. The words are dictated in the context of given sentences and arranged in age-specific sets which are informed by the NLS. Fifteen seconds are allowed for the candidate to write each word which gives a useful indication of spelling fluency.

- **Wechsler Individual Achievement Test – 2nd UK edition for Teachers (WIAT-II-UK-T) (4 – 85:11 years)**

A single word spelling accuracy test is included with the WIAT's reading assessments. It is useful across a wide age range, provides standardised scores and covers letter-sound correspondence and well as regular and irregular words, contradictions and high-frequency homonyms.

- **Wide Range Achievement Test – 4th edition (WRAT- 4) (5 – 94 years)**

The WRAT4 spelling subtest also gives an indication of spelling fluency by allowing 15 seconds for each word to be written. There are parallel forms – blue or green and a combined version - so care is needed to use the correct norms.

See also **Dyslexia Portfolio** (page 89) – this is a combined test including both literacy and processing skills.

N.B.: Specialist Teachers working with Psychologists may also have access to the BAS & WORD spelling tests, but cannot purchase these resources themselves.

Free writing

Form 8: Section C
Question 3 continued

Spelling difficulties, very slow speed of writing or extremely poor readability – both handwriting and composition – might warrant an arrangement to allow candidates to show what they know. Thus, free-writing by hand and free-writing using computer support are all necessary aspects of the assessment. Other samples of the candidate's free-writing under controlled conditions (such as the latest end of year exam papers) might also be useful for comparison. All free-writing tasks should be **timed**, so that questions about writing speed can be answered.

> Evidence from a sample of free writing can be used to contribute to an application for a **scribe, extra time, transcript[23], word processor***

(*see discussion below on use of word processors)

In regard to free writing the JCQ asks the following:
- Does the candidate's spelling and / or handwriting render his free writing largely illegible?
- Is the candidate's free writing incomprehensible?
- Is the candidate proficient in the use of a word processor?

Many candidates with dyslexia cannot sustain the same level of accuracy or legibility when their attention is focused on composition rather than spelling – especially under time constraints. Apart from spelling and handwriting, they may have such significant difficulties with composition – at sentence and text level – that their writing becomes "incomprehensible".

Samples of free-writing should therefore be analysed qualitatively as well as quantitatively and the percentage of illegible words due to poor handwriting or bizarre spelling calculated. Learning support teachers are usually rather good at deciphering dyslexic students' spelling – so try to put yourself in the shoes of the English, science or geography examiner! Clearly a high number of "unrecognisables" here is very telling with regard to the quality of a

---

[23] From September 2011 a transcript will become a Centre-awarded arrangement.

candidate's spelling – whereas if your answer is 0% – then the examiners will not have a problem reading this candidate's scripts. Some of the options to consider are:

- Can the student produce an altogether more readable level of written output when using a word processor? This is a crucial question to answer as **it is much preferred that candidates work independently**.
- If, even when using a computer, the candidate's writing is still "incomprehensible" or still so slow extra time makes little difference, can he express himself orally and dictate his ideas – either to a human scribe or through voice-input software?
- Is a transcript the best solution if the student is not proficient with a keyboard and a teacher who knows the student can decipher the writing?

Word Processing

The use of a word processor – with no spell check or other support facilities enabled – can now be awarded to a candidate without specialist evidence of need and the request does not need to be recorded using JCQ systems (AAO or paper-based). **However, the JCQ do not intend that this means any student who wants a laptop in their exam should have one. A candidate should not simply be given a word processor because he uses a laptop/computer at home or prefers to type rather than write.** If he were this could go against the principle that no arrangement should give any candidate an unfair advantage. This might be the case if he has no underlying difficulty and can type faster than his peers across the country can write by hand.

> To award a word processor the Centre should ask if this truly represents the candidate's normal way of working. Does he use a keyboard most of the time for study activities, and in some or all exams and timed tests? Are some or all lessons supported this way?

Where the use of a word processor is being considered Patoss recommends that Centres should **continue to investigate the candidate's speed and quality of writing when using a word processor**. This will help maintain a professional, evidence-based approach to verify that no unfair advantage is being conferred and establish if a need for extra time remains, and if so, how much.

When investigating if extra time is needed when working with a word processor the following scenarios, among others, could arise. The candidate might:
- express his ideas more easily using a word processor such that the quality of language now represents what he knows. If he also types at the same pace as others handwrite no extra time is given.
- type at the same average speed as his peers handwrite, but because he faces additional difficulties with speed of processing and organising his writing he is awarded some extra time. The usual evidence for extra time is required.
- type faster than average standards for handwriting – in this case he already has an advantage regarding time, which he can use to proof-read and edit his responses, so no extra time is given.

Although many people with learning difficulties do prefer to type, some do not, and assessors should check before requests are made.

> Remember: Use of a word processor with predictive text and spell check facilities switched on requires the same level of evidence as a scribe[24].

Writing Speed

Form 8: Section C
Question 4

Written output may be meagre for many reasons – problems with expressive language, composition, spelling or manual dexterity (or all of these).

A standardised score for **writing speed** is strongly recommended where age appropriate test materials are published but a "**words per minute**" measure is also acceptable evidence for:

- A scribe
- Up to 25% extra time.

Where a "words per minute" measure is used the assessor should confirm the writing rate is below national standards, not simply those of his peers at the Centre.

Under the current regulations, where awards of **more than 25% extra time** are considered appropriate to compensate for writing speed difficulties a **standard score of below 70** on a writing speed **and/or** processing test is required.

When evaluating free writing samples against standardised scores it is crucial to use appropriately matched data. This is because the test tasks can vary so much from one another and so produce different results. So, **you cannot administer one type of task and then use the norms from a different one to assess free writing speed.**

Free writing tasks of 20-30 minutes duration were used to assess handwriting speeds of Y10/11 pupils in research projects by Penny Allcock[25] and Liz Waine[26] carried out in large comprehensive schools. Both found a wide range of "average" writing rates (means of 15/16 w.p.m. with a SD of 5). These findings are at variance with those reported in the DASH manual (see below). This might be accounted for by students having different guidance in the choice of topics to write about and the shorter DASH writing task (10 minutes). This difference in writing task is crucial and assessors might like to think about which is the best measure for their students.

> NB. Copying tasks or dictation exercises cannot get to the heart of writing speed issues. These tasks do not provide the required measure of free writing speed as they do not include that vital element of composition. (They may be qualitatively useful to

---

[24] Note differences in regulations for Functional Skills.
[25] Allcock, P. (2001) "Testing Handwriting Speed" Patoss website: www.patoss-dyslexia.org
[26] Waine, L. (2001), "Writing Speed: what constitutes slow?" In Rose, R. & Grosvenor, I. (Eds) *Doing Research in Special Education – Ideas into Practice* London: David Fulton

compare performance with free writing and identify the precise problem being faced by the student but this would fall into the "other information" category.)

Writing Speed: Test Resources

> These tests may be used to contribute to evidence for a **scribe, extra time**

- **Allcock Assessment of Handwriting Speed[27] (Year 9 – 11, with projected scores Year 12 – 13)**

This downloadable test uses a 20 minute free-writing task and the administration and scoring data are described on the Patoss website where research results are also given. Allcock has calculated the cut-off points at which candidates should be allowed 25% extra time in order to have equal opportunities compared to "average" candidates to finish written answers, or might need a scribe. She has also predicted average free-writing speeds during Y12 & Y13 by projecting scores from the 2001 data.

- **Detailed Assessment of Speed of Handwriting (DASH) (9 – 16:11 years)**

For group or individual administration this fully standardised test takes about 30 minutes and includes 5 component tasks. Standardised subtest and composite scores are provided. Tasks 1- 4 cover perceptual motor competence, copying quickly and in "best" handwriting and writing out the alphabet. Task 5 is a 10-minute free writing task with a choice of 12 writing topics. A pilot study was undertaken to ascertain the topic and methodology which produced the "best results" - i.e. the most words, and comparison of words per minute (wpm) produced in response to two different titles gave statistically different results. This is an extremely important fact to remember and is, no doubt, part of the reason why the average raw scores and norms obtained here differ significantly from those using Penny Allcock's methodology. Normative data across the UK was collected in tandem with the re-standardisation of the *Movement Assessment Battery for Children.*

- **Detailed Assessment of Speed of Handwriting – (DASH 17+) (17 – 25 years)**

DASH 17+ can be administered individually or in a group. Again, it takes about 30 minutes and includes the 5 component tasks described above.

N.B: The **Hedderly Sentence Completion Test** has been purposefully **excluded** here as it does not assess free writing skills, although it may reveal students with moderate to severe difficulties at word and sentence levels. The norms are now somewhat outdated and this test is best used for qualitative purposes.

---

[27] Free to download from Patoss website

Other Relevant Information

Here is the assessor's opportunity to record any other details which will assist the Centre and Awarding Bodies in making a decision about access arrangements.

For reading difficulties, such information should help to clarify whether an individual reader or access to a reader in a group is needed, if read aloud is the preferred option, or if an oral language modifier, or extra time (10%, up to 25%, or more) is the most effective arrangement.

In the case of writing difficulties, this information should help in deciding if extra time (10%, up to 25% or even more in exceptional cases), dictation to a scribe, use of a word processor or provision of a transcript would be the most appropriate arrangement?

Cognitive processing difficulties identified through formal testing are reported in this section, together with a brief note about their likely impact in examinations. Tests of **phonological skills, verbal memory, processing speed and visual/motor skills** are likely to prove useful to evidence underlying difficulties. You might also report here underlying general ability measures if these are relevant to the application.

> In exploring these "other " areas of need the pattern of difficulties presented by some candidates will mean that the proper course of action is to refer him to a practitioner with different skills and resources. An important aspect of responsible professional practice is recognition of the limits of one's own area of expertise.

In this section, please keep your comments focused on salient issues and succinct.

Extra time

The award of extra time, while the most common arrangement, actually requires some of the most detailed investigation and clarity of evidence to come to a fair conclusion for all – both those who genuinely need extra time and all the other exam candidates who would probably like some! (For some example cases see Chapter 10 and Chapter 3 – Borderline Cases.)

The JCQ requires "more than one" type of evidence to support this arrangement – one specialist test will not cover it – and decisions need to be made about the appropriate amount of time or whether a supervised rest break might meet the need.

Have you considered a supervised rest break? This might be better for some candidates who suffer concentration difficulties or extreme exam stress.

Have you considered the 10% extra time option? This might be sufficient for some candidates.

There remains a great deal of confusion about extra time. Firstly, it is important to say that all candidates applying for extra time because of a learning difficulty must have been assessed by a Specialist Teacher or qualified Psychologist within the secondary or FE phase of education or have a Statement of SEN relating to secondary education. In addition to these specialist assessments, supporting evidence can come from noting the candidate's working patterns in class and in completing homework.

> *Please note, candidates whose need for extra time arises from a medical, physical or psychological concern have different evidence requirements.*

To be awarded extra time the overwhelming majority of candidates will have **below average scores** in relevant cognitive processing measures and/or below average reading and writing speeds. However, these below average scores are not *always* necessary if a significant impact on the candidate's ability to demonstrate their knowledge and skill can be demonstrated.

In 2010 the JCQ established guidance that "low" standardised scores in processing speed and/or reading or writing speeds were acceptable evidence for up to 25% extra time. From September 2011, this will be further clarified to indicate that:

Below average scores (SS less than 85) in relevant processing measures and/or below average reading and/or writing speeds will be needed for the overwhelming majority of candidates to qualify for up to 25% extra time.

However, in *exceptional cases* "low average" scores (SS 85 – 89) *might* be used to contribute to an overall picture of need if a significant impact on the candidate's ability to demonstrate their knowledge and skill can be demonstrated. If these low average scores are used the JCQ requires Centres to provide a compelling, clear and detailed picture of need with a substantial weight of evidence to demonstrate difficulties. A single low average result is **not sufficient.**

This flexibility to use "low average" in addition to "below average" (84 or less) scores will be especially useful for highly able candidates with SpLDs who have developed their skills through hard work, good teaching and use of compensatory strategies. While their literacy skills are good, their cognitive processing speed measures might still fall within the low average range. Specialist teachers will need to investigate whether these **cognitive processing** scores are **substantially lower** than measures of their other skills and abilities. Professional judgement and skill and an overall view of individual cases will be required when evaluating if differences are "substantial".[28] In these instances there may be a case for up to 25% extra time to compensate – often allowances of 10% will help individuals overcome residual difficulties and be sufficient to meet their needs The assessor can advise the Centre, taking note of the current regulations. The Centre can then decide if it is

---

[28] See Chapter 9 for discussion of the interpretation of score differences.

appropriate for the student. This will be the case if they regularly use such time – and the need may be particularly noticeable in stressful situations like exams.

This evidence of a specialist assessment, or a Statement of SEN, will still have to be substantiated by evidence of normal way of working and current need: unfinished mock exams or timed assessments, IEPs / ILPs, or a compilation of observations from teaching / learning support staff showing a clear **need** for extra time.

Phonological Skills: phonological awareness and processing speed

• **Comprehensive Test of Phonological Processing (CTOPP) (5 – 24:11 years)**

This American test contains many subtests and covers a wide age range. It is reasonably quick to administer although some parts of the test require a CD to be played. The core subtests provided for older students (1 – 6) would normally be used in this context; they provide standardised scores for phonological awareness, phonological memory and rapid naming skills. However, supplemental tests can be used for further evidence if necessary - the supplemental rapid naming subtests – colours and objects – can be particularly useful to demonstrate difficulties of working at speed.

Please note the mean on the subtests is 10 and the standard deviation is 3. The scores are also given as percentiles. These percentiles can be converted to standardised scores using the manual of any other standardised test manual as these are fixed points on the normal distribution curve.

• **Dyslexia Portfolio (6 – 15:11)**

Given the age range of this resource is unlikely to be very widely used by those assessing for access arrangements, but it may be useful in some instances. This test straddles the divide between individual and computerised assessment, providing standardised scores but also allowing important qualitative analysis. Measures are provided in word level spelling, reading and written productivity (by means of a copying test for the very young and free writing for older students). A group of diagnostic cognitive processing tests address rapid naming skill, reading speed, working memory and phonological skills and these also provide standardised scores. To generate its final report the programme assumes that data about underlying general cognitive ability is available; this should be preferably drawn from individually administered, recent and reliable tests. While the programme produces guidance from the results, it is necessary for assessors to take into account their own observations and conclusions before producing a report.

• **Phonological Assessment Battery (PhAB) (6 – 14:11 years)**

The ceiling on this test is quite low for our purposes, so will only be useful for a very small number of candidates. The picture naming, fluency and spoonerisms tests will challenge older students with severe phonological deficits so might be used qualitatively.

- **Perin's Spoonerism Task (14 – 25 years)[29]**

This test was originally standardised for Y10 students, and was considered useful for older students. However, its norms are now quite out of date. It is perhaps best used as a qualitative indicator of difficulties and other standardised measures of phonological skills employed. Timing is crucial and the time to be recorded is from when the tester finishes dictating the two words until the candidate finishes his response, viz.

Tester, "Sue Lawley" Start timing …… Candidate, "Loo Sawley" Stop timer

Time Taken

Memory Skills

- **Digit Memory Test (6 years – adult)[30]**

This quick to administer test provides a standard score. Digits must be read out to the candidate in a monotone at 1 second intervals. Research has shown that deficits in verbal memory (the phonological loop of working memory) are almost universal in dyslexia. In this test, should the length of the sequence of numbers recalled on digits backwards be markedly lower than forwards - that is an unusually large difference in the "string" of numbers recalled - this may indicate a particular difficulty in "working memory". A difference of 3 or more is considered worthy of note.

- **Wide Range Assessment of Memory and Learning – 2nd edition (WRAML-2) (5 – 90 years)**

This individual test is a comprehensive investigation of memory skills, covering both immediate and delayed recall of verbal and visual information, with 6 subtests in the core battery. It generates a general memory index but also useful visual, verbal, working memory and attention/concentration composite standardised scores. Administration time can be up to one hour. A subset of the core battery can be used for screening and additional tests are available to interpret core findings more fully.

- **Automated Working Memory Assessment (AWMA) (4 – 22 years)**

This is a computer-based assessment of working memory skills, both auditory and visual. There are three levels of assessment - a screener (5 – 7 minutes), a short form (10 –15 minutes) and a long form (around 45 minutes). The test sequences are pre-set and standardised test scores based on UK populations are calculated; some guidance on how the working memory profile will affect learning is also provided. The ability of the assessor to quickly and accurately input the student's responses, as well as the sound quality are crucial to the reliability of the results.

---

[29] Free to download from the Dyslexia Action website – for full location reference see Chapter 13
[30] Also, free to download from the Dyslexia Action website – see Chapter 13

Additional Tests of Reading Skills

These tests cannot generally be used to support the award of a reader on their own but may be useful to contribute to the overall evidence base for other arrangements.

- **Hodder Oral Reading Tests (HORT) (5 – 16+ years)**

As well as providing a single word test useful for a reading accuracy measure the further subtests in this battery can prove useful. The sentence reading test allows investigation of the degree to which the candidate's mechanical word recognition skills are supported by grammar and meaning at sentence level. The reading speed section assesses how many regular three and four-letter words the candidate can read in 60 seconds and thus focuses on "automaticity" of lower-level reading skills and could provide additional evidence to back up text-level reading speed measures.

- **Nonword Reading Test (NWRT) (6 – 16 years)**

First developed in Australia and then standardised in the UK in tandem with the Diagnostic Reading Analysis & the Edinburgh Reading Test - 4, this test has 2 parallel forms and provides error analysis columns on the record sheets to help identify phonic patterns the student does not know and needs to learn.

- **Test of Word Reading Efficiency (TOWRE) (6 – 24:11 years)**

The TOWRE yields valuable information, and standardised scores, about how **automatically** (i.e. quickly) the candidate can read words, often a factor in comprehension difficulties. It compares both real word and non-word reading under **timed** conditions. A discrepancy between the two subtest scores is particularly revealing. Dyslexics are often far worse at the non-word subtest due to their weak decoding skills.

- **Wordchains (7 – 18 years)**

This efficient way of assessing word-level skills in a group is useful for screening as well as individual use. It assesses **silent** word recognition by asking candidates to put lines where the boundaries are in strings of words printed without spaces between them. As it is not measuring the same skills as a traditional reading test it can only be used in this category of providing additional information. The manual contains data showing correlations between Wordchains scores and grades achieved at Key Stage 3 & GCSE English and English Literature. The Letterchains section can also be used to screen for visual-motor skill deficits.

Visual Processing Speed / Visual-Motor Skills

The impetus to assess visual / motor skills may well come from concerns about reading accuracy, reading fluency, handwriting legibility and handwriting speed.

- **Beery-Buktenica Developmental Test of Visual-Motor Integration - 6th Edition (2-100 years)**

The 6th edition of the Beery provides three subtests. All three sections can be used or just one or two of the subtests to give standardised scores for visual and motor performance. A below average score for visual-motor integration and/or visual perception can indicate difficulties in visual tracking and a low score for motor coordination a difficulty with fine motor control and/or the ability to focus on the page.

- **Letterchains (7 – 18 years) (Part of the Wordchains test)**

The Letterchains section of Wordchains can be used to screen for visual-motor skills deficits.

- **Morrisby Manual Dexterity Test (14 years - adult)**

The Morrisby can be a useful test (quick to administer and cheap to buy!) for demonstrating significant problems with fine motor skills.

- **Symbol Digit Modalities Test (SDMT) (8 years - adult)**

Quick to administer, this test measures facility with printed symbols, and is considered to be substantially a visual processing speed test, although other skills are needed. Valuable information can be gathered by comparing performance on the written and oral subtests and expose any motor control difficulties. Standard scores can be calculated from the manual, although they are not provided in a table.

General Underlying Ability

Since "appropriate entry" is the Centre's responsibility and will to a large extent depend on each candidate's teacher's assessment of attainment in that subject, psychometric assessment of general ability is not usually needed in this context. There are always cases, however, where either the Centre – or very often the candidate – has a "need to know" when considering a particular course of study.

The tests listed below measure two components of ability - verbal and non-verbal reasoning. They are often referred to as measures of "general underlying ability". However, as they represent simply two facets of ability Patoss does not recommend they are referred to as tests of intelligence or their scores labelled as measures of IQ. (A full ability profile also includes cognitive processing abilities and these are crucial in a diagnostic assessment to determine if an SpLD is present. Cognitive processing includes measures of phonological skills, memory skills and phonological and visual processing speeds – tests are listed earlier in this chapter, in the "Other Relevant Information" section.)

Scores from verbal and non-verbal reasoning tests can add weight to an argument for access arrangements, such as extra time, if they provide clear evidence of significant contrasts in the candidate's wider profile of cognitive skills or their literacy attainments.

> **However, it is important to note that discrepancies between verbal and/or non-verbal test results and literacy scores are not sufficient on their own either to diagnose an SpLD or to argue for access arrangements. Additional evidence from testing of cognitive processing skills is essential.**

Group Ability Screening - some considerations

In some cases information about learners' underlying ability may already be available in schools from the results of tests, for example the Cognitive Abilities Test (CAT). However, some caution is needed in their use.

Results of group underlying ability tests can be misleading for a variety of reasons for students with SpLDs. They are designed as screening tests to provide only a brief measure of non-verbal and/or verbal ability. Students with SpLDs may be disadvantaged due to weak literacy skills, the style of the response sheet, processing speed weaknesses, attention or concentration problems and indeed the overall level of student motivation in taking such a test.

Some colleagues, if they are less familiar with the impact of SpLDs, place a great deal of trust in these ability results. This can lead to lower expectations, or confirmation of a teacher's view that weak performance is due to a lack of ability. However, the Specialist Teacher can play an important role here: if after careful examination of results (taking into account history, background and other professionals' views), and where there is an uncertain result, individual ability testing is strongly recommended.

It should be remembered that studies have generally shown relatively low correlations of 0.4 to 0.6 between IQ test results and exam grades, so we should never underestimate the contribution that good teaching and hard work can make to educational attainment, nor overestimate the significance of IQ/ability scores!

General Underlying Ability Tests

These tests are *not required* for access arrangements but assessors might find them useful to contribute to an overall profile of a student.

- **British Picture Vocabulary Test - 3rd Edition (BPVS-III) (3 – 16 years)**
The BPVS is a test of receptive vocabulary. This new, fully revised edition includes colour pictures and improved presentation. It has been re-standardised by the National Foundation for Education Research (NFER) using a large UK sample. It is also a useful resource since norms for students whose first language is not English are available, which may be helpful when considering the need for a bilingual dictionary. However, some candidates will be near to the ceiling of this test. Therefore alternative resources (see below) may be preferable.

- **Expressive Vocabulary Test - 2nd edition (EVT- 2) (2:06 – 90 years)**
This revised edition of the EVT is co-normed with the Peabody Test (see below) making direct comparisons possible. It is relatively quick to administer, provides parallel forms and a computer programme to calculate scores.

- **Kaufman Brief Intelligence Test: 2nd edition (K-BIT) (4 – 90 years)**
An individually administered test, re-standardised in 2004, which includes two verbal ability tests – receptive and expressive language skill – and one non-verbal test – matrices, which together provide a composite ability score.

- **Naglieri Nonverbal Ability Test (5 – 17 years)**

Stemming from the older Matrix Analogies Test, this is a useful resource with students who have language difficulties or EAL. In addition it has minimal motor requirements and is designed to be unbiased for students with impaired colour vision, although it relies heavily on visual skills so this should be borne in mind when interpreting results. Administration time is 30 minutes.

- **Peabody Picture Vocabulary Test - 4th edition (2: 06 – 90+ years)**

Quick to administer (10 – 15 minutes) this wide age range resource measures receptive vocabulary for standard English and provides one indicator of verbal ability. Two parallel forms are provided. Several changes have been made to this revised edition of the Peabody, providing a more accessible format and aiming to provide a better range of words.

- **Ravens Progressive Matrices and Vocabulary Scales (7 – 18 years)**

This well-known test, which measures non-verbal and verbal aspects of ability, has been re-standardised for the UK and redesigned, simplified and updated – with the new edition published in 2008. The layout of the multiple-choice format of the response sheet may be tricky for some students - those with dyspraxia or visual tracking problems.

- **Wide Range Intelligence Test (WRIT) (4 – 84 years)**

Widely used by Specialist Teachers in the UK, the WRIT contains four sub-tests which measure verbal and visual abilities. Anglicisation of a number of items from the American original have been authorised by the publisher[31]. The scores can be aggregated to give general, verbal and visual ability measures, although consideration must be given to reliable use of composite scores, as in all tests. (See Chapter 9: Composite Scores for more detail.)

Screening Tests

This chapter has thus far noted the main tests available to support access arrangements. These lists specifically **exclude screening tests** as this type of test is not sufficient for the purpose of access arrangements. They are, of course, very useful in a number of other ways – but they are not recommended for this purpose.

Well-established screening resources include:
- Dyslexia Screening Test – Secondary
- Dyslexia Adult Screening Test
- Dyslexia Screener
- Lucid Adult Dyslexia Screener (LADS)
- Quick Scan
- A range of other attainment tests are also often used as screening materials, for example Hedderly, Suffolk Reading Scale Digital (2nd edition).

---

[31] These can be supplied to qualified test users by Patoss or Dyslexia Action

Lucid Exact (11 – 24 years)

This is a computerised assessment of a range of literacy skills. It tests word recognition, reading comprehension (accuracy and speed), spelling and speeds of handwriting and typing from dictation. Test administration is carried out by computer and begins with spoken instructions and practice items. It takes between 30 – 40 minutes. The programme calculates standardised results, although the administrator must mark the handwritten dictation.

Lucid Exact suggests it is the ideal solution to assessment for access arrangements but **in our view** this is not necessarily the case. While the programme could contribute to understanding a student's profile it does not *appear* to provide comprehensive information for an access arrangement assessment. There are a number of points which the assessor should bear in mind:

- The word recognition test is timed and therefore not suitable for use in this context. This is noted in the Exact manual. 6 single words are presented for 5 seconds in a random position on the screen, one of which is dictated. Using the mouse, the student must click on the correct word. Success on this test may therefore be compromised by difficulties with hearing, visual tracking and / or manual dexterity. It does not reflect the exam task well. To meet JCQ regulations further testing in single word reading (untimed) would be necessary.
- Typed responses in the spelling test rely on accurate keyboard skills.
- The five reading comprehension passages escalate sharply in level of difficulty. Assessors will need to assure themselves that the texts are suitable for their particular cohort, especially at the lower and upper age range.
- The JCQ regulations require quantitative and qualitative assessment of free writing skills, but the hand written and typed dictation tasks in this test are insufficient for this purpose. Although a slow speed on the handwriting and typing dictation tasks will indicate difficulties with either skill, as well as spelling, the composition element of writing is missing. The standardised results would at best provide only supplementary evidence for access arrangements and further testing would be necessary to fulfil JCQ requirements.
- Exact is designed for independent use but where teachers suspect students may not be motivated to complete it thoroughly, or may be easily distracted, closer supervision will be necessary to obtain reliable results.

This software has been subject to a fuller Patoss review due to be published later this year. Concerns about the validity, usefulness and cost of this tool have been raised (See Backhouse, McCarty and Green, 2011[32]) and schools and colleges may wish to consider these issues before deciding if Exact is appropriate for them.

As with all other screening resources, Patoss recommends that Exact is not entirely relied upon for access arrangement purposes.

---

[32] Backhouse, G, McCarty, C and Green, L. (2011) **Forthcoming**. *Lucid Exact: An Evaluation* Patoss Bulletin, Summer 2011 Vol. 24 Issue 1

Finalising Your Report

- Carefully check your marking and standard scores
- Check you have all necessary information regarding a candidate's case history, history of provision and normal way of working
- Complete your pro-forma summarising all the evidence
- Complete Section C of Form 8 if appropriate
- Proof-read your work
- Present your findings to the SENCO / ALS Manager.
- Ensure you have established, or have confidence in, systems which inform the candidate and his teachers of the outcome of the assessment.

Access arrangements assessments are a perfect opportunity to investigate the wider learning support needs of students. By identifying the individual's strengths and weaknesses, the assessor can use results and observations to help design learning support plans and guide subject teachers and tutors on ways to facilitate learning in class, and thus help candidates to become more effective, confident and independent learners.

Student Record Sheet - Access Arrangements

Name of Candidate:			DoB:		Year of Entry:
Date of Assessment:			Chron. Age:		Candidate Number:

Section A, History of Need				Section C, Profile of LDs		
History of difficulties				Reading Skills		
Level on CoP				1. Reading Accuracy		
KS 3 NCT scores:	E	M	Sc	Name of test		
				Test ceiling		
Previous Assessment? Y/N	By whom?			Date of admin		
				S.Score		
Screening Tests				Reading age		
Name of test	Score			Comments		
				2. Reading Speed & Comprehension		
				Name of test		
				Test ceiling		
Learning Support?				Date of admin		
				Speed wpm		
Previous Access Arrangements? (Date & Exam)				Speed S.S.?		
				Compreh S.S.	Set time	ET
				Comments		
Normal way of working:				Writing Skills		
National Curriculum Levels				3. Spelling assessment		
Subject:	Level:			Name of test		
				Test ceiling		
				Date of admin		
				S.Score		
				% unrec words		
				Comments		
				4. Writing Speed		
				Free wr, wpm		
				% unrec words		
				Dict/WP wpm		
				Quality of lang		
Section B, Recommendations				Other relevant info		
1						
2						
3						
Student's comments:						

Caroline Read 2007   This sheet can be photocopied without infringing copyright.

Table for comparing results on assessment

Student's Name: ....

Date tested: ....   Assessed by: ....

Standardised Test Results

Standard Deviation	-3	-2	-1	0	+1	+2	+3
Standardised score	<70	70 - 84	85 - 89	90 - 110	111 - 115	116 - 129	130>
Description	Well below average	Below average	Low average	Average	High average	Above average	Well above average
Test							

Other Test Results / Notes

Test	Result / Comments (relationship to average performance)

Patoss 2011: This sheet can be photocopied without infringing copyright

9. Basic Concepts in Psychometrics

In this section, you will find a brief summary of some of the most important issues you must understand when choosing, using, scoring and interpreting the results of standardised tests in an educational setting.[33]

There are two main types of standardised test:

1. Maximum performance – where the candidate has to do the best he can, e.g. single word reading tests.
2. Typical performance tests – which assess how the candidate generally behaves, thinks, feels, etc., such as questionnaires.

For assessment of learning difficulties tests of maximum performance are usually used.

Choosing Standardised Tests

Test manuals vary regarding the amount of technical information they give. The contents range from basic facts to a large amount of complex statistical information generated during the test development and standardisation. The amount of work involved in gathering this data is very considerable and the reason why tests are expensive.

> N.B. You should be very wary of tests developed by individuals or small organisations that may not have the financial resources or expertise to support the proper development of tests.

The Standardisation Sample

Every time we look up an individual's test results in norm tables, we are in effect comparing his performance with that of the group used during the test development and standardisation. The larger that group and more widely distributed across different areas (inner city, suburban, rural, etc.) the more likely it is that the statistics regarding what is average, above and below, are meaningful and 'true' for the population as a whole.

Furthermore, since language, literacy standards and other attributes within both school and general populations are constantly evolving norms established several decades ago may not be fair representations of the population now.

Action: Choose tests which have been recently standardised on a large, nationally representative sample.

---

[33] This chapter is abridged and edited from Backhouse, G and Morris, K (2005) *Dyslexia? Assessing and Reporting, the Patoss Guide* Hodder Murray: London

The **age range** of the standardisation sample is also extremely important – particularly during the primary school age range when development of skills and knowledge is much faster than later on. This is why tests usually provide separate norm tables for each 6 months during the early school years, then expand the age groups to 1 year in the secondary phase and as abilities 'plateau' in adulthood they are given 5 or 10 year bands thereafter. For statistical reasons, tests do not discriminate well at the extremes of their age range and so best practice is to use tests for individuals whose ages are well within the test 'ceiling' and 'floor'. (Please see below in regard to age equivalent scores and reporting scores when using tests above their ceiling.)

Action: Choose a test which more than covers the age range of the students you are assessing.

Reliability

The reliability of a test reflects the extent to which it consistently measures the target skill(s). There are many ways of assessing reliability, each with its own advantages and so reliability is not a fixed quantity. You will find details of the methods used in each test in its manual.

Data about the **internal reliability** of a test is usually represented by reliability coefficients. The reliability coefficient (r) indicates what proportion of the test variance is due to 'real' individual differences. The higher the reliability coefficient of a test (1.0 = perfect reliability although this is never achieved), the more confidence may be placed in the consistency and precision of the results it generates.

Action: Look for reliability values above 0.8 and preferably above 0.9. The lower the reliability, the less confidence you can have concerning the candidate's real ability based on that particular test result.

An often-quoted measure of internal reliability is known as Cronbach's Alpha. This checks to see what proportion of the candidates get questions of differing difficulty correct. For example only the best should get the hardest ones correct. Values over 0.8 indicate well-designed and balanced tests that should enable differentiation to occur.

When all the items in a test are 'operating' (i.e. not too difficult or too easy) then the more items there are in a test, the greater its reliability. Therefore the results of short tests – in terms of number of items – should never be relied upon in a formal assessment, without a great deal of complementary and supporting evidence.

> N.B. Although a test such as the TOWRE[34] may be short in terms of time taken but the number of items to be read is high, which is the crucial factor. This contributes to high reliability coefficients.

---

[34] Test of Word Reading Efficiency

A number of computer based tests now screen individuals to ensure they only do questions of appropriate difficulty. This has the advantage of not wasting time and effort on too easy or too hard questions while still maintaining reliability by ensuring a minimum number of items are included. In a multiple-choice test this minimum should be 30, pitched at around the appropriate level.

Other important aspects of test reliability are:

Test-re-test Reliability: Candidates should obtain the same scores if they take the test on 2 separate occasions.

N.B. In the assessment context, retesting within a short period of time is likely to produce a higher result due to learning that occurred during the first trial and so is not recommended.

Administrator / Inter-scorer Reliability: The same results should be obtained no matter who is administering or marking the test when using the standardised delivery as specified in the test manual.

Action: Choose tests with high reliability coefficients and a good number of items to be tackled by the candidate.

Validity

Validity studies tell you to what extent the test measures what it says it does and has to be considered in the context of what the test user needs to know. Again, there are different ways of measuring validity because there are different aspects. The main ones are:

Concurrent validity shows that people who are already known to differ on the task being measured, obtain correspondingly different scores on the test.
E.g. on a clerical aptitude test do good clerks score well and bad clerks score poorly?

Predictive validity can be used to tell what will happen in the future.
E.g. Do IQ tests predict exam grades?

Content validity relates to the how well the test covers all relevant aspects of the skills being measured.
E.g. Does an untimed single word reading test measure 'real' reading ability – the capacity to read text with full comprehension straight away?

Much information regarding validity is expressed in terms of correlations with results of other similar tests, exam results, teachers' ratings, studies with special groups and so on.

Correlation coefficients

Correlation coefficients express the relationship between two variables, but do NOT necessarily mean that one causes the other – although it may.

For example, there is a very high correlation between children's reading ability and the size of their feet – they both increase with age (the underlying factor), but neither causes the other!

> **Action**: Choose a test which focuses on and measures the *precise* skills you wish to investigate. Select tests that provide sound evidence of their validity for the purpose.

Using Standardised Tests

A principal characteristic of standardised tests is that administration procedures, stimulus materials and scoring are prescribed, are exactly the same for all who use and take them and match precisely the method used when the test was standardised. Since all candidates have (as near as possible) the same test experience, differences in scores should therefore reflect true differences in ability.

> **Action**: Make sure you know and follow the precise procedures for administration of any test that you use. The manual will usually tell you the exact words to use and whether (for example) you may repeat a question.

Understanding Test Scores

Most tests of ability and attainment, if administered to a large, representative sample of the population, produce roughly bell-shaped (normal) distributions, with lots of people scoring in the middle/average range (the 'central tendency') and far fewer having extreme (very high or very low) results.

The scales are usually converted so that every test has the same **normal probability curve** – a smooth symmetrical frequency curve having known mathematical properties.

Raw scores (direct numerical reports of performance, e.g. 60/85 on a test) are converted to derived scores – showing each person's relative position, compared to his peers, by using norm tables.

There are 3 types of derived scores:
- **Standardised or Standard Scores**
- **Percentile Scores**
- **Age Equivalent Scores**

Standardised Scores

These show the candidate's position relative to the mean for his age group; the **mean** is the arithmetical average score for the reference group.

The **standard deviation** (SD) is the average deviation from the mean – regardless of direction. Scores within 1 SD either side of the mean on any test are classified as 'average' (often further sub-divided into 'low average', 'average' and 'high' average).

If a **normal distribution** is 'sliced' into vertical bands 1 SD wide, a fixed percentage of cases always falls into each band and the overwhelming majority will fall within 3 SDs either side of the mean. The largest proportion of individual scores is 'bunched up' in the middle band (1 SD either side of the mean).

Approximately two thirds (68%) of individuals will fall in the 'average' range, defined in this way (34% either side of the mean). See Fig. 9.1.

> **Standard scores are the most appropriate type of derived score to use when considering a candidate's results.**

Standard scores indicate how far away from the average level an individual is in terms of actual performance on a test. Furthermore, by measuring this distance in terms of standard deviation units, we can compare an individual's performance on one test with his results on another and derive a profile of strengths and weaknesses – as well as see how well he matches up to his peers.

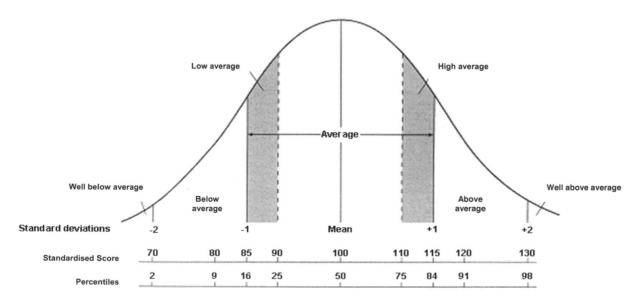

Fig. 9.1 The Normal Distribution Curve, standard deviations & percentiles

Figure 9.2   Hypothetical example

Say we measured 1000 adult women and found their average height to be 5 ft. 5 ins.

How would we then define *below average* (short) and *above average* (tall), and how many women might be expected to fall into these categories?

This is where the standard deviation is useful since it is a measure of the *variance*, in relation to the *mean* and is a generic mechanism for defining the above and below average 'benchmarks' on any standardized scale.

By finding the deviation (difference) from the mean of all 1000 women:
(e.g. if height = 5 ft. 2 then deviation from mean   = 3 ins.
    .. ..   = 5 ft. 7   ..   ..   ..   = 2 ins
    .. ..   = 5 ft. 5   ..   ..   ..   = 0 ins
         & etc.)

the *standard deviation* can be calculated by applying a set formula to the results obtained from the sample. Let us suppose the SD turned out to be 2 inches.

We can now define (statistically) the average range as between 5 ft. 3 ins. and 5 ft. 7 ins. and expect roughly 680 out of every 1000 women (68%) to fall between these limits. We can also define what we mean by above and below average in terms of height and using the SD (of 2 ins.) can predict that only 20 women are likely to be under 5ft. 1 in. and another 20 above 5 ft. 9 (2 SDs above & below the mean) using our knowledge of percentile.

Mean =	5 ft. 5 ins.
Standard deviation	2 ins.
Above average (+1 SD)	5 ft. 7 ins. (16% of popn.)
Below average (-1SD)	5 ft. 3 ins. (16% of popn.)
Well Above average (+2 SDs)	5 ft. 9 ins. (2% of popn.)
Well Below average (-2SDs)	5 ft. 1 ins. (2% of popn.)

As for percentiles – it is now relatively easy to see why they can be misleading. Out of our 680 average height women many are likely to be almost or exactly 5ft 5ins. It is clearly a nonsense to call someone who is 5ft. 4½ short, or another of 5ft. 5½ tall. You would be hard pressed to notice the difference between them and might easily misjudge who was the taller, even though one might be at the 35th percentile (5ft. 4½) and the other at the 65th (5ft. 5½). This sounds like a huge difference – but in terms of 'raw scores' is in fact negligible in relation either to each other, or to the mean.

If, however, we think in terms of SD units (of 2 ins.) we can say one is taller than the other if there is at least 2 ins. between them; or one is below average if she is 5ft. 3 or under.

Percentile Scores

These reflect the percentage of the group whose scores fall below that of the candidate. A 10th percentile rank is therefore a low result (90% would do better) and a 90th percentile rank is pretty good as only 10% would exceed this score.

There is relatively little difference between the raw scores of a large percentage of individuals whose results are near the mean. Thus percentile scores between 16 & 84 are 'within the average range'.

Percentile scores therefore can magnify small differences near the mean which may not be significant; and reduce the apparent size of large differences near the tails of the curve i.e. the difference, in terms of actual performance, between percentile ranks of 5 & 15 is far larger than that between percentile ranks of 40 & 50. Standardised scores avoid this since the intervals on a standardised scale are all equal – but they are not generally well-understood by non-specialists. See hypothetical example in Figure 9.2.

Age Equivalent Scores

The third type of derived score is the age equivalent. This tells you the chronological age, or age range, for which an individual's raw score is average. However, age equivalents become less and less appropriate as the age of the candidate increases, since the rate of development of skills and attainments slows. This is illustrated in the table below concerning two pairs of learners.

7 year old learners	A difference of 1 word read on the TOWRE (Sight Word Efficiency) by two 7 year olds only alters the Age Equivalents by 3 months. The Standard Scores are within the average range for both and the Age Equivalents reflect this.
16+ learners	Contrast this with a 24 year old reading just 2 less words than a 16 year old. The age equivalents are roughly the same for both learners, but the 24 year old's looks very low, 9 years below his actual age. However, his standard score is within the average range for his age group (as it is for the younger student), because the norms at 16 are remarkably similar to those at 24.

Chronological Age	Raw score	Standard score	Age Equivalent
7 yrs. 0 mths.	31	98	7 yrs. 3 mths.
7 yrs. 6 mths.	30	91	7 yrs. 0 mths.

16 yrs. 6 mths.	92	98	16 yrs. 0 mths.
24 yrs. 6 mths	90	91	15 yrs. 6 mths.

> **It is recommended that age equivalent scores be avoided altogether. Certainly age equivalent scores should not be used for secondary or adult candidates.**

If, for some reason, age equivalents are required for someone in this older age group, you should take great care to explain any large discrepancies between age scores and chronological age.

Interpreting Test Scores

So long as we know the mean and standard deviation of any standardised scale, we can interpret a student's performance in relation to others in his age group, also his own score on other tests. For both purposes, it will lead to sounder conclusions if standard deviation units, rather than percentile scores are used. Some common standard score systems are given in the table, but in the UK most tests now report a derived score using a mean of 100 and this is often called a quotient:

	Mean	Standard Deviation
Stanines (e.g. NARA, CAT[35] tests)	5	2
T-scores (e.g. BAS)	50	10
Deviation Quotients (e.g. WRIT[36]; PhAB[37], BPVS[38])	100	15
Wechsler IQ & CTOPP subtests	10	3

Confidence Intervals and Standard Error of Measurement

Confidence intervals (or confidence bands) provide a range of test scores within which we can be confident that the "true" measure of the candidate's skill lies. These ranges are calculated using the standard error of measurement (SEM).

There is always the possibility of a discrepancy between a person's 'true' and obtained score because of the imperfect reliability of any test. (Psychological testing is not an exact science!) The SEM is the likely size of this discrepancy and confidence intervals are based on SEMs. There is an inverse relationship between the reliability coefficient of a test and its SEM. A highly reliable test will have a small SEM and so each obtained score is likely to be close to the hypothetically 'true' one.

Most test manuals provide data regarding standard errors of measurement (SEM) and confidence intervals (bands) – either in the norm tables (e.g. NARA II[39]) or in the chapter about test reliability (e.g. CTOPP[40]). Many manuals publish tables giving the confidence interval directly but if they do not it can be calculated from the SEM data.

---

[35] Cognitive Ability Tests
[36] Wide Range Intelligence Test
[37] Phonological Ability Battery
[38] British Picture Vocabulary Scales
[39] NARAII Neale Analysis of Reading Ability; second revised British edition
[40] CTOPP Comprehensive Test of Phonological Processing

Confidence intervals are usually defined thus:

- it is 68% certain that a person's 'true' score will be within the band of scores lying 1 SEM either side of his obtained score. This is the 68% confidence interval.
- it is 95% certain that it will be within plus/minus 2 SEMs of his obtained score.
- it is 99% certain for the range 3 SEMs either side.

The 95% confidence interval is the one most commonly used in specialist teacher reports.

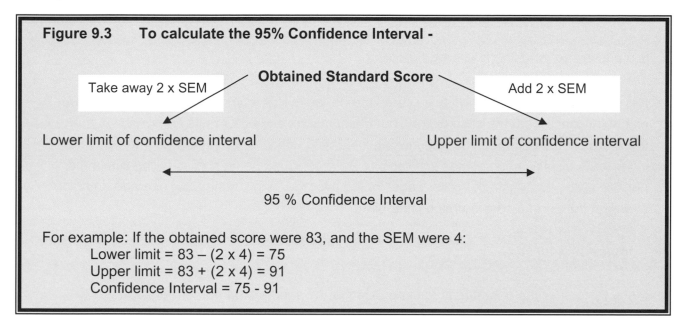

Figure 9.3   To calculate the 95% Confidence Interval -

Take away 2 x SEM

Obtained Standard Score

Add 2 x SEM

Lower limit of confidence interval

Upper limit of confidence interval

95 % Confidence Interval

For example: If the obtained score were 83, and the SEM were 4:
        Lower limit = 83 – (2 x 4) = 75
        Upper limit = 83 + (2 x 4) = 91
        Confidence Interval = 75 - 91

Significance and Probability

Test manuals also provide information about the significance of the results given as Probability coefficients (p). These tell you about the likelihood of getting a particular result, or set of results, by chance. The smaller p is, (e.g. 0.05, 0.01, 0.001) the more significant the result; i.e. it would have been very unlikely to have occurred by chance.

However, the finding that a score is unlikely to have occurred by chance does not *necessarily* make it a rare, and thus diagnostically useful, result and further professional consideration is needed.

Language used to describe scores

Different test publishers use a variety of verbal labels such as 'low average',OCR 'superior' and so forth to describe different sections of the normal curve, which can be confusing. By far the safest thing to do, especially in the context of access arrangements, is to stick to the statistical divisions based on standard deviations, as this reflects the JCQ approach. This would lead to the following:

Score	Label
131 or more	Well above average
116 – 130	Above average
111 - 115	High average
90 – 110	Average
85 - 89	Low average
70 - 84	Below average
69 or less	Well below average

'Low average' and 'high average' scores

It is often the case that certain test scores are not quite in the below average range and yet all the evidence from the case history, our observations and other tests convinces us that there are sufficient grounds for diagnosing a learning difficulty. Given the degree of error inherent in tests it is *sometimes justifiable* to base conclusions on scores falling within the narrow 'slice', just within the outer edges of the average range, called low average and high average, but careful consideration is required.

Composite Scores

Many tests offer the opportunity to bring together the scores on a number of sub-tests to provide a combined measure of a skill. In many cases the composite score is more reliable than the sub-test scores as they bring together related skills. ***However***, if statistically significant differences exist between subtest scores, calculation of a composite has the potential to hide any underlying strengths and weaknesses and it may mask some elements of the spiky profile which we are seeking to explore when investigating SpLDs. Thus, where statistically significant differences exist between any pairs of scores it is better not to calculate, or report, the composite score to which they contribute.

Consider the following examples:

Example 1: Test of Word Reading Efficiency (TOWRE)		
Subtests: Sight Word Reading	112	
Phonemic Decoding	75	
If the difference between these two scores were ignored a composite score for the Total Word Reading Efficiency of 92 would be obtained. However, this hides the very useful piece of information regarding a significant weakness in phonemic decoding.		

Example 2: Wide Range Intelligence Test (WRIT)			
Subtests: Vocabulary	98	Matrices	95
Verbal Analogies	101	Diamonds	74

In the WRIT the vocabulary and verbal analogy scores can be combined to provide a "verbal ability" measure and the matrices and diamonds results combined to provide a "visual ability" score. However, in this case the latter is not recommended. The difference of 21 points between the matrices and diamonds results is statistically significant for this particular individual and the combined score could hide the student's detailed profile.

Action: Consult test manuals for data giving the magnitude of difference required between two scores to establish statistical significance.

Interpreting Score Differences

In order to establish if statistically significant differences exist across test scores a **conservative** approach can be adopted using the 95% confidence interval.[41]

If there is to be the possibility of a *real* difference between two scores the lower limit of the confidence interval around one score should not overlap with the upper limit of the other – that is the confidence intervals should be clear of one another.[42] Where this gap exists between the confidence intervals this tells us a statistically significant difference exists and indicates further investigation of the difference is warranted. Assessors should be aware that where confidence intervals overlap at the very extremes of the range there might also be cause to investigate further.

However, please remember that a statistically significant difference simply tells us the score discrepancy did not occur by chance. Nothing more. Further professional consideration is required to establish if a difference is unusual, improbable or rare in comparison to the rest of the age-matched population and large enough to be reflected in everyday activities. This requires professional judgement and consideration of the whole profile. Some test manuals provide data on rarity but others do not. As a very general guide a difference of *at least* 1.5 standard deviations between test scores is considered necessary to exclude simple statistical test variation and to move towards consideration that the difference may be unusual with an impact on everyday life.

Reporting scores when using tests above their ceiling

Given the increasingly wide range of test materials available selecting a test appropriate to the age of the candidate is becoming easier. However, if you have assessed a student whose chronological age is higher than the test ceiling (e.g. the CTOPP with a 27 year old) great caution must be exercised. In such cases qualitative descriptions of his performance

---

[41] See confidence interval discussion above and Figure 9.3
[42] Turner, M (2004) *An Introduction to the Theory and Practice of Psychological Testing* in Turner, M and Rack, J (Eds) The Study of Dyslexia; Kluwer Academic Publishers, London

should be given in the report avoiding statistical language. However, there are occasions where assessors feel it is imperative to provide numerical evidence of their findings. Here, you should consider the likelihood that the ceiling performance will be reliable for the older age group. Where such scores are used, report readers must be made aware that the test was used beyond its ceiling and be provided with an explanation of the subsequent reliability issues.

Ipsative testing

This term is used when a profile of individual strengths and weaknesses is based on comparison of a person's scores on different tests. Conclusions about his differential abilities, learning difficulties, attainments and so-on are drawn on the basis of contrasts of one or more standard deviations between standardised scores on different tests.

> N.B. Although it is generally acceptable to compare standard scores from different tests caution should be exercised if the two tests were standardised on very different populations or at different times, e.g. 1970 vs. 1990 – a generation apart.

The difference between a 'deficit' and a 'discrepancy'

Differences in a learner's profile are a key factor in assessment but we must be careful to distinguish between deficit and discrepancy; a deficit refers to only one domain or skill, a discrepancy goes across domains.

> **Returning to our hypothetical example** - would it be reasonable to say that women measuring 5ft. 3ins. have a problem? Clearly not! However, being 5ft. 2 (1.5 SDs below the mean) may begin to affect life on the odd occasion. One's vision is restricted in crowds, choice of some clothes restricted to those available in 'Petite sizes' and it's hard to reach things off higher shelves – nothing serious, but a nuisance at times. At 2 SDs or more below the mean the difficulty falls into the deficit range (5ft. 1 and below in this hypothetical example) as more everyday things may become difficult – standard kitchen equipment is uncomfortably high and some careers – where there are minimum height requirements – are barred.

It remains to be said that 'deficits' are defined in relation to the mean and the demands made on the ability/characteristic measured. Height, for example, is only an issue in certain situations.

When comparing results across tests you will find that few people perform at the same level in every test administered to them.

A candidate may get well above average marks on a verbal test and an average score for non-verbal reasoning. He is likely to find language-based subjects easier than practical ones. The difference of 2 SDs between scores is highly meaningful regarding his potential strengths and weaknesses. However, he cannot be said to have a 'deficit' in non-verbal reasoning as the lower score is not in the deficit range. He may well have a problem, however, if he chooses to study technical or scientific subjects at advanced levels.

However, his scores suggest there is a 'discrepancy' between his verbal and non-verbal ability and this is one piece of evidence in drawing up a full profile of an individual which will eventually lead to a diagnostic decision. In terms of an SpLD a statistically significant and rare discrepancy between verbal and non-verbal ability is helpful, but not at all conclusive evidence of an SpLD.

10. Case Studies

The case studies which follow are drawn from 'real life' or common scenarios. Permission to use the details given has been given, although names have been changed. These examples have been chosen and updated to demonstrate a range of needs and briefly illustrate the process of gathering the evidence required before appropriate decisions can be made about access arrangements. (See also brief examples in Chapter 3- Borderline Cases.) Further examples are given by the JCQ which is **the primary reference**.

Case Study: Jamie (Year 10 – taking GCSEs)

Reason for referral: Jamie's parents are concerned about his apparently different results in tests over homework and coursework; Jamie reports never being able to finish exams.

Background: Jamie is a high achieving student who has had no additional support at school. However, he has received 1:1 tuition privately for several years. Teachers confirm Jamie often runs out of time in class tests.

Assessment results:

Standardised score	<70	70 - 84	85 - 89	90 - 110	111 - 115	116 - 129	130>
Description	Well below average	Below average	Low average	Average	High average	Above average	Well above average
Test							
WRAT 4 – single word reading					115		
WRAT 4 - spelling				110			
TOWRE - composite			86				
WRAT E - Comprehension						125	
CTOPP Rapid Naming	52						
CTOPP Alt rapid naming	69						
Beery – Motor co-ordination			89				
Allcock – Free writing		10.5wpm					
Free writing – word processed			17 wpm				

Test	Result / Comments (relationship to average performance)
Allcock Handwriting	% undecipherable words – 0.5% Quality – age appropriate, good spelling, organisation

Recommendations following assessment:
- Use of word processor – spell check disabled
- Up to 25% extra time – monitored for possible request for over 25% extra time

Discussion:
Jamie is very happy using a word processor and typing helps him overcome some of his speed difficulties. However, underlying processing difficulties still exist, evidenced in well below average CTOPP tests, and low average Beery and TOWRE results contribute to the

picture of need. The TOWRE results are particularly noticeable given the substantial difference between these and the WRAT4 result. Taken together these results might have been used to recommend over 25% extra time, as in current JCQ regulations processing speeds below 70 are accepted as evidence. However, Jamie and his teachers feel 25% is appropriate so a decision is taken to monitor performance and review.

Case Study: John (Year 10 – taking GCSEs)

Reason for referral: John was assessed because of extreme difficulties with writing and he reported finding reading very tiring.

Background: John is a high achieving student who was diagnosed with severe dyspraxia in Year 4 and has two psychologist reports on file. Although he can type he is very slow so TA's have worked with him in class and teachers have scribed for him during all school tests, and his parents for homework. He is used to dictating his work and does so fluently. The SENCO needed a specialist assessment to support an application for a scribe for all exams and she wished to explore reading difficulties.

Assessment results:

Standardised score	<70	70 - 84	85 - 89	90 - 110	111 - 115	116 - 129	130>
Description	Well below average	Below average	Low average	Average	High average	Above average	Well above average
Test							
WRAT 4 – single word reading					114		
TOWRE – sight words		78					
TOWRE – non words		79					
Edinburgh 4				97			
Edinburgh 4 + 25% extra time					112		
WRAT 4 – spelling 25% unrecognisable		84					
Free Writing - by hand 50% unrecognisable		7 wpm					
Free Writing - dictated						25 wpm	
Free Writing - word processed		5 wpm					
Digit Memory Test			85				
CTOPP Rapid Naming				90			
CTOPP Alt rapid naming			88				
CTOPP Phonological awareness				91			
WRIT – General ability composite						125	

Test	Result / Comments (relationship to average performance)
Free writing	John's handwriting is incomprehensible and he was visibly distressed and tired when asked to write by hand. He had no difficulty continuing his composition by dictation however which was well structured and used age-appropriate language.

Recommendations following assessment:

- Scribe
- Up to 25% extra time (For use in papers that require significant reading)

Discussion:

The assessment supported the school's view that the use of a scribe whenever possible was the best arrangement to support writing. His word processing skills are too weak to make that approach a viable option. For formally assessed coursework, as his parents will not be allowed to scribe as they have previously, John will use a Dictaphone and a TA will type up work completed at home and return it by e-mail attachment for him to edit. However, John was strongly advised by the assessor to learn how to use voice-activated word processing to foster independence.

The reading assessments showed that his accuracy at word-level was excellent but his reading efficiency was weak – his results on the TOWRE were below average. Also, although his reading comprehension was average, given 25% extra time he was able to improve his score by a full standard deviation. Taking these results together it was agreed that extra time of up to 25% for papers requiring a good deal of reading would be reasonable.

Case Study: Shelley
(Part-time student at an Adult Education College – taking GSCE in English)

Reason for referral: Shelley's tutor had become concerned that although she was "extremely conscientious" and her skills were improving she had significant difficulty with spelling and speed of reading and writing.

Background: Shelley's schooling was frequently interrupted due to her mother's long-term illness. She was late to speak, read and spell and found it very difficult to study and write essays when older. Shelley has received very little learning support, and her word processing skills are very limited. She is a qualified Nursery Nurse and has achieved NVQ 2 & 3 qualifications with literacy support. She has attended Basic Skills classes for 3 years and is working towards a GCSE in English which she will need to further her career.

Assessment results:

Standardised score	<70	70 – 84	85 – 89	90 – 110	111 – 115	116 – 129	130>
Description	Well below average	Below average	Low average	Average	High average	Above average	Well above average
Test							
WRAT 4 – single word reading	67						
WRAT E - Comprehension			87				
WRAT 4 – spelling 20% unrecognisable		82					
Free Writing speed by hand 0% unrecognisable		11 wpm					
TOWRE – sight word reading		76					
TOWRE – non-word reading	55						
Digit Memory Test		75					
CTOPP Rapid Naming		70					
WRIT – Verbal				93			
WRIT – Nonverbal			86				

Recommendations following assessment:

- Up to 25% extra time – to be monitored in mock exams
- Read Aloud

Discussion:

Shelley's reading accuracy at word level is below average and her non-word decoding under time pressure is particularly weak (TOWRE). She tackled the reading comprehension test confidently but when offered extra time to finish the test Shelley refused saying that it was "getting too hard".

Her spelling was below average and although she made logical and recognisable attempts at familiar words her attempts at unknown words were not phonically regular. Her free writing, although slow, was legible. She used words she felt confident about and mistakes were minor. Her written style was simple but well expressed.

The cognitive tests revealed very weak phonological processing (CTOPP rapid naming) and weak verbal memory (Digit Span) but a normal level of general underlying ability.

The results, at face value, would support an application for a reader and scribe, and for extra time. However, Shelley's normal way of working is by herself; albeit slowly. She can read by herself and write legibly. She had no desire to be 'helped' in any way and she wanted to be assessed 'properly'. She felt it would be fair if she had extra time and when the Read Aloud option was explained to her she felt this would be helpful and would not be considered 'cheating'.

Case Study: Emma (Year 10 – following GCSE and Entry Level courses)

Reason for referral: Emma was referred for assessment due to her history of learning difficulties and to support an application for both a reader and scribe.

Background: Emma has a statement of SEN (Year 5) due to moderate learning difficulties. She received daily small group support until Year 5 when weekly support was put in place by the Local Authority and continued until Year 9. Emma currently works in a small, low ability group and a TA is available to help with reading, writing and comprehension. At Key Stage 3 Emma took part in Teacher Assessment only and achieved: writing 2c; reading 2a; spelling 2. She was absent on the day of the maths test but achieved a Level 4 in the science test. Emma was allowed a reader, scribe and additional time and although she made good use of the reader and scribe she did not use the extra time in the science test.

Assessment results:

Standardised score	<70	70 – 84	85 – 89	90 – 110	111 – 115	116 – 129	130>
Description	Well below average	Below average	Low average	Average	High average	Above average	Well above average
Test							
WRAT 4 – single word reading	62						
Graded Word Spelling 5% unrecognisable		72					
Allcock handwriting speed 5% unrecognisable				14 wpm			
Free writing speed - dictated						24 wpm	
CTOPP Rapid naming (letters and digits) Alternate rapid naming		76 76					
CAT– Verbal		72					
CAT – Nonverbal		70					

Recommendations following assessment:

- Reader and scribe

Discussion:

Emma's single word reading score (WRAT4) was very low and she found the test quite distressing. It was clear that further testing of reading comprehension would not be helpful at this assessment. However, this score was sufficient evidence to request a reader.

Her free writing was quite fluent but much of it was difficult to read due to handwriting, spelling and grammar difficulties, and Emma did not use a word processor often. In contrast, when dictating to a scribe her speed increased and the content, though still fairly basic, was easy to understand. This was how she often worked with the TA. This difference and her below average spelling score supported the request for a scribe – although the assessor recommended continued practice with a word processor.

Emma's results in the CTOPP processing speed tests could be used as evidence of need of extra time. However, although allowed this time in class tests Emma had never used it. She often completed papers well within the time allowed having answered all she could.

After discussion between the specialist assessor, SENCO and class teacher it is decided to not to request extra time as the experience of staff who knew Emma well was that she would not be able to use it.

Case Study: George (Year 10 - taking GSCEs)

Reason for referral George's English teacher has concerns about his spelling and feels his handwritten work does not reflect his ability.

Background: George has a well-documented history of difficulty with learning. He has received language therapy and occupational therapy. A psychologist's assessment in primary school identified some difficulty with attention and in processing spoken language. Parental and school information pointed to mild evidence of inattention at home and impulsivity at school, but no difficulties with completing work within time allowed were reported.

Assessment results:

Standardised score	<70	70 – 84	85 – 89	90 – 110	111 – 115	116 – 129	130>
Description	Well below average	Below average	Low average	Average	High average	Above average	Well above average
Test							
WRAT 4 – single word reading					114		
WRAT 4 – spelling				104			
Free writing speed - by hand- DASH. 0% unrecognisable				105 24wpm			
Free writing speed - word processed				25wpm			
TOWRE – sight word reading					112		
TOWRE – non-word reading				102			
Digit Memory Test				110			
CTOPP Alternate Rapid Naming			89				
SDMT - written				107			
BAS II – Verbal						120	
BAS II – Nonverbal						125	

Recommendations following assessment:

- Word Processor
- Use of prompter / rest breaks to be considered during class tests and application made if subsequently appropriate.

Discussion:

George has received a great deal of learning support for literacy throughout his schooling; he continues to receive individual support, focusing on written composition. His single word spelling is at an average level and in his free writing all errors were recognisable in context. His writing speed is virtually the same when using a word processor as it is when writing by hand. However, the main difference between the two pieces of work was that the vocabulary he used in the word-processed piece was much more sophisticated and better reflected his spoken vocabulary and verbal ability. George routinely uses a computer in school and it is his normal way of working.

Although there is a significant difference between George's performance on a number of these tests when compared to his general ability level, all the results are within the average range. It was considered that the use of a word processor would help George demonstrate his knowledge more aptly but that an extra time allowance was not justified.

11. Frequently Asked Questions

These questions are all drawn from those most commonly received at Patoss and the JCQ. In all cases further guidance can be found in earlier chapters and the JCQ regulations. They are listed under themes.

Extra Time

1. What evidence is required for extra time?

See Chapter 8 for discussion. In summary you should have:

- A formal Statement of Special Educational Need relating to secondary education **OR**
- Evidence of below average processing speeds and/or reading or writing speeds from a specialist assessment conducted by an appropriately qualified Specialist Teacher or Psychologist **PLUS**
- Evidence of current need – this evidence can vary widely but could include an IEP / ILP showing need for extra time, evidence from mock exams or timed tests, or a compilation of observations from teaching and learning support staff confirming need for extra time.

Processing and/or reading or writing speeds should be in the below average range in the overwhelming majority of cases. However, if a substantial and weighty picture of need can be built there are rare circumstances where a low average speed might be used as one piece of evidence to contribute to this picture. **However, one low average processing speed score would certainly not be sufficient in any case.** In these cases, the Centre and the specialist assessor would need to clearly show why there was a need for extra time and provide detailed and compelling evidence to demonstrate it.

2. What is the best test for extra time?

It depends! A selection of useful cognitive processing tests are listed in Chapter 8: Other Relevant Information. These are tests of memory skills, phonological skills, and speed of processing measures. We would recommend tests of reading speed using **continuous text** and/or **free writing** speeds as very useful in all cases. It is highly likely that more than one test is needed to firmly establish the need.

3. When can I use a "low" score for extra time?

Below average scores should be used to substantiate extra time requests. However, you can use "low average" scores (SS. 85 – 89) when you have a substantial weight of evidence that shows the need for this extra time – one low average score by itself is not sufficient. See question 1 above. The use of low average scores should be considered an exception and the Centre would have to provide a clear and detailed justification for the candidate.

4.   Do I need a standardised score for reading or writing speed for 25% extra time?

Access arrangements online does not require entry of a standardised score for the award of up to 25% extra time. However, you are advised to record standardised scores wherever an up-to-date, nationally standardised, age appropriate test is available. In other circumstances a words per minute score is acceptable, particularly in the case of writing speed, as long as the specialist assessor confirms this represents a low score compared to national standards, not simply standards in the Centre.

5.   Can I give extra time for exam stress?

No. You should teach exam management strategies and offer supervised rest breaks instead. If the candidate also has learning difficulties which impact on his speed of working and these are exacerbated by stress these would be very good grounds for extra time.

6.   Do I need an assessment by a Specialist Teacher or Psychologist when only extra time up to 25% is needed?

Yes. A report written in the secondary or FE phase of education, or a formal Statement of Educational Need will meet this requirement.

7.   Where does the school stand in regard to privately commissioned reports by a Psychologist or Specialist Teacher which recommends extra time?

The Head of Centre can decide to accept or reject the recommendations of the report. Any rejection would not be based on a dispute of the diagnosis made by the professional but on the lack of evidence of current need within the Centre and/or if the degree of difficulty experienced does not meet JCQ regulations.

If the private report is accepted, the Head of Centre must note, and take copies of, the assessor's qualifications and formally record their rationale for the acceptance of the report.

We recommend open and early communication with candidates, and their parents where appropriate, to encourage joint working with the Centre to avoid such situations if at all possible.

8.   Can a student have extra time as well as a reader and/or scribe?

Only if you can demonstrate why they need the extra time as well as the other arrangement – it is not an automatic right. You would have to provide all the evidence required for extra time and show the need persisted even when using the reader and scribe.

9.	**Can I give extra time to a highly able dyslexic candidate who has a discrepancy between his verbal and non-verbal ability, or between his ability and literacy skills even when these are all well within the average range?**

No. Extra time is only awarded to those with low processing or reading/writing speeds regardless of discrepancies between their other abilities.

Readers and Reading Skills

10.	**My student has reading accuracy, comprehension and speed scores in the low average range – can he have a reader?**

No. For the award of a reader below average standard scores (84 or less) are required in accuracy OR comprehension OR speed. They cannot have an individual reader or access to a reader in a group without meeting the "below average" criterion.

11.	**My student does not qualify for a reader – what can I do?**

If all scores (reading accuracy, comprehension or speed) are 85 or above but you feel there is a need for support you could consider the following arrangement options:
- Use of read aloud – reading aloud to themselves helps some learners to spot their own accuracy mistakes and improve their comprehension
- Modified paper or modified language paper – an exam paper with enlarged fonts might help some learners, an exam paper with the carrier language made more accessible might help others. Trial the options with past exam papers and see if these are helpful before ordering.

These both are Centre-awarded arrangements where no specialist evidence is required. You could also investigate to see if extra time helps this learner.

12.	**Can bi-lingual candidates have a reader?**

No. Only those who also have problems in their own language and evidence of learning difficulties and a history of need and provision can be considered.

13.	**Can students use computer reading programmes instead of a member of staff acting as a reader?**

A computer is only acceptable where the candidate is entirely familiar and happy using the reading software and has been using it regularly. Also, as part of the role of a reader is to read back to the candidate what they have written you must consider if that need is applicable to the exam in question.

**14.	How many students can I put in a group to have access to a reader?**

This should be determined by the needs of the students – JCQ say the group should be no more than 4. You should ensure the students are not operating at very different levels such that one candidate dominates the reader to the exclusion of access for the others and consider if the students are actually confident enough to put up their hand and ask for help.

Scribes and Writing Skills

**15.	What are the criteria for a scribe?**

A "scribe" suggests either: a human scribe, use of voice input software or use of a word processor with the spell-check facility enabled. You must have at least one of the following:
- A below average standard score on a single word, un-timed spelling test
- A below average standard score OR words per minute rate in free writing speed
- Evidence of incomprehensible writing
- Evidence of entirely illegible writing

Plus, all the usual evidence history of need and current way of working.

A helpful route is to compare the candidate's independent free writing with that produced using a computer and a human scribe. If he struggles to get his ideas down and produces only a few lines of barely legible script when unaided compared to a whole page of age / course appropriate text using support then a scribe is clearly the right option. The Centre can retain copies of this assessment evidence in SEN / ALS files – and simply note these findings for the JCQ inspector – they no longer need to see the samples directly.

**16.	How can I decide which scribe arrangement to choose?**

You should opt for the arrangement which gives the candidate the most independence, *which still allows him to fully demonstrate his knowledge*, and which he is confident in using. You should consider them in this order of preference: (1) Word processor (2) Voice-input system (3) Transcript 4) Human scribe.

**17.	Can a scribe use a word processor?**

Yes. This may negate a need for extra time if the scribe types quickly.

**18.	What is the school's position if a candidate demands to use a word processor, or they have a private report stating that a word processor is their normal way of working?**

A word processor should be awarded where this is the current way of working for some or all of the course, and/or where all or most of exams and tests are taken using a word processor. You do not have to provide a word processor simply because a student prefers to work that way. The relevant evidence to normal way of working is that which is observed in the Centre.

19. **Can students bring in their own laptops for the exams?**

No. All word processors used must meet JCQ set up guidelines.

20. **Is some interpretation allowed in transcripts?**

No. The transcript must be a word for word copy of the candidate's script as the purpose is simply to provide a legible copy of what the candidate has written. Spelling correction is only allowed of non-technical words and word order should not be altered.

Other

21. **Is verbal / non-verbal ability testing necessary?**

These types of tests are not required for access arrangements. A discrepancy between verbal and non-verbal underlying ability scores is not sufficient for an access arrangement of itself. These scores might, however, be helpful for painting an overall picture of students' needs, especially in borderline cases where such data may add to the weight of evidence.

22. **How do colleges obtain history of provision and evidence of current need?**

If a candidate declares a difficulty on application or enrolment, you can request a copy of his existing evidence, or get permission from him to contact his previous school. If this is not forthcoming or simply not available, you will have to base your application on the student's reported experience alongside Centre screening, individual specialist assessments and staff observations over the first term at college (see Chapter 6) and carefully list the provision that will be made for him over the period of his current course. By the time of the exam this will then have become his history of provision and now his normal way of working.

23. **What arrangements are available for students diagnosed with dyscalculia?**

The diagnosis itself, as with dyslexia, does not bring any automatic arrangement and a calculator, which is the common request, is only permitted where it is also available for all candidates to maintain the validity of the qualification. A discrepancy between literacy and maths test results is not sufficient to argue for an arrangement. If cognitive processing speed difficulties exist you might be able to argue for extra time for maths / numeracy exams. However, please consider whether this is useful for the individual – it might just be making the torture of the maths exam even longer if they do not have the strategies in place to help them use the extra time.

12. Test Information

The following pages provide a quick reference to the tests mentioned earlier in this book. Further commentary is given in Chapter 8.

Tables are presented under:

- Reading – including accuracy, comprehension and speed (Figure 12.1)

- Writing – including free writing and spelling (Figure 12.2)

- Cognitive Abilities – including general underlying cognitive ability and cognitive processing ability tests. Also visual motor skills. (Figure 12.3)

All tests are listed in alphabetical order under these headings.

Approved tests for use in assessments to support Disabled Students Allowances applications are also identified. These are tests formally approved at present. Updated lists of approved tests are posted on the Patoss website as they become available.

In the table the column **Use**:
- I denotes tests administered on an individual basis
- G denotes those that can be administered in a group.

Please note that those without specialist qualifications cannot conduct tests to support access arrangements. For test data to be used as access arrangement evidence the specialist has to sign to confirm that she carried out all the tests.

Figure 12.1: READING SKILLS

Please see Chapter 8 to identify which tests can be used to support a particular access arrangement.

*Use: I denotes individual; G denotes group test administration

Name of Test / Where and when published	Age Range	Use*	Skill	Page	DSA
Access Reading Test UK / 2006	7 – 20+	I / G	Silent sentence and text level reading comprehension	79	
Adult Reading Test (ART) UK / 2004	16 – 25+	I	Oral text level reading accuracy, reading rate and comprehension	78	✓
Diagnostic Reading Analysis – 2nd edition (DRA) UK / 2004	7 – 16:05	I	Oral text level reading accuracy, reading rate and comprehension	78	
Dyslexia Portfolio UK / 2008	6 – 15:11	I	Single word reading (also tests some writing and cognitive processing skills)	89	
Edinburgh Reading Test – 4 (ERT4) UK / 2002	11 – 16	I / G	Silent sentence and text level reading comprehension	80	
Edinburgh Reading Test 4 – Interactive (ERT4i) UK / 2002	11:7 – Adult	I	Silent sentence and text level reading comprehension	80	
Gray Oral Reading Tests – 4th edition (GORT 4) USA / 2000	6 – 18:11	I	Oral text level reading comprehension	78	✓
Gray Silent Reading Tests (GSRT) USA / 2002	7 – 25	I / G	Silent text level reading comprehension	80	✓
Hodder Group Reading Tests – New Edition (HGRT) UK / 2007	5 – 16+	I / G	Word, sentence and text level reading comprehension	80	

Name of Test / Where and when published	Age Range	Use*	Skill	Page	DSA
Hodder Oral Reading Tests (HORT) UK / 2006	5 – 16:09	I	Single word reading, sentence reading and reading speed	76 91	
Nonword Reading Test (NWRT) UK / 2004	6 – 16	I	Phonemic decoding	91	
Single Word Reading Test (SWRT) UK / 2007	6 – 16	I	Oral single word reading	76	
Test of Word Reading Efficiency (TOWRE) USA / 1999	6 – 24:11	I	Reading efficiency for single sight words and non-words	91	✓
Wechsler Individual Achievement Test – 2nd UK edition for Teachers (WIAT-II-UK-T) UK / 2006	4 – 85:11	I	Single word reading accuracy, text-level reading comprehension and reading speed (also tests spelling)	76 79	✓
Wide Range Achievement Test – 4th edition (WRAT- 4) USA / 2006	5 – 94	I	Single word reading accuracy, sentence level reading comprehension (also tests spelling, arithmetic)	81	✓
Wide Range Achievement Test – Expanded (WRAT-E) Individual Form USA / 2001	5 – 24:11	I	Reading comprehension – text level (also tests maths, nonverbal reasoning)	79	✓
Wide Range Achievement Test – Expanded (WRAT-E) Group Form USA / 2001	7 – 18:11	G	Silent reading comprehension – text level (also maths; nonverbal reasoning)	80	✓
York Assessment of Reading for Comprehension – Passage Reading Secondary UK / 2010	11 – 16	I	Text level reading accuracy, comprehension, reading rate	79 81	

*Use: I denotes individual; G denotes group test administration

Figure 12.2: WRITING SKILLS

Please see Chapter 8 to identify which tests can be used to support a particular access arrangement.

*Use: I denotes individual; G denotes group test administration

Name of Test / Where and when published	Age Range	Use*	Skill	Page	DSA
Allcock Assessment of Handwriting Speed UK / 2001	School Yr 9 – 13	I / G	Free writing speed + qualitative evaluation of writing	86	
Detailed Assessment of Speed of Handwriting (DASH) UK / 2007	9 – 16:11	I / G	Free writing speed, copying speed (best and fast), graphic speed, alphabet writing speed + qualitative evaluation of writing	86	
Detailed Assessment of Speed of Handwriting (DASH 17+) UK / 2010	17 – 25	I / G	Free writing speed, copying speed (best and fast), graphic speed, alphabet writing speed + qualitative evaluation of writing	86	
Diagnostic Spelling Tests (3 – 5) UK / 2006	9 – 25+	I / G	Single word spelling	82	
Dyslexia Portfolio UK / 2008	6 – 15:11	I	Single word spelling (also tests some reading and cognitive processing skills)	89	
Helen Arkell Spelling Test (HAST) UK / 1998 (Test being re-standardised at time of writing)	5 – 17+	I	Single word spelling	82	✓
Vernon Graded Word Spelling Test - 3rd edition UK / 2006	5 – 18+	I / G	Single word spelling	82	
Wechsler Individual Achievement Test – 2nd UK edition for Teachers (WIAT-II-UK-T) UK / 2006	4 – 85:11	I	Single word spelling (also tests single word reading, comprehension)	82	✓
Wide Range Achievement Test – 4th edition (WRAT- 4) USA / 2006	5 – 94	I / G	Single word spelling (also tests single word reading, sentence comprehension)	83	✓

Figure 12.3: COGNITIVE ABILITIES

Please see Chapter 8 to identify which tests can be used to support a particular access arrangement.

*Use: I denotes individual; G denotes group test administration

Name of Test / Where and when published	Age Range	Use*	Skill	Page	DSA
Automated Working Memory Assessment (AWMA) UK / 2007	4 - 22	I	Working memory (visual and verbal)	90	
Beery-Buktenica Developmental Test of Visual-Motor Integration - 6th edition (BEERY VMI) USA / 2006	2 – 100	I / G	Visual motor integration, visual perception, visual-motor skills	91	✓
British Picture Vocabulary Test - 3rd edition (BPVS III) UK / 2009	3 – 16	I	Receptive language	93	
Comprehensive Test of Phonological Processing (CTOPP) USA / 1999	5 – 24:11	I	Phonological awareness, phonological memory, phonological processing speed (rapid naming)	89	✓
Digit Memory Test UK / 2004	6 – Adult	I	Short-term and working verbal memory	90	✓
Dyslexia Portfolio UK / 2008	6 – 15:11	I	Rapid naming skills, phonological skills, working memory (also tests some reading and writing skills)	89	
Expressive Vocabulary Test - 2nd edition (EVT-2) USA / 2007	2:06 - 90	I	Expressive language	93	
Kaufman Brief Intelligence Test – 2nd edition (K-BIT) USA / 2004	4 - 90	I	Receptive and expressive language, nonverbal reasoning	93	
Morrisby Manual Dexterity Test UK / 2003	14 – Adult	I / G	Visual-motor skills and manual dexterity	92	✓

Name of Test / Where and when published	Age Range	Use*	Skill	Page	DSA
Naglieri Nonverbal Ability Test USA / 2003	5 – 17	I / G	Nonverbal reasoning	94	
Nonword Reading Test (NWRT) UK / 2004	6 – 16	I	Phonemic decoding	91	
Peabody Picture Vocabulary Test - 4th edition USA / 2007	2:06 – 90+	I	Receptive language	94	
Perin's Spoonerism Task UK / 1983	14 – 25	I	Phonological awareness	90	
Phonological Assessment Battery (PhAB) UK / 1997	6 – 14:11	I	Phonological awareness, phonological fluency, phonemic decoding, phonological processing speed	89	
Ravens Progressive Matrices and Vocabulary Scales UK Norms / 2008	7 – 18	I / G	Verbal and nonverbal reasoning	94	
Symbol Digit Modalities Test (SDMT) USA / 1982	8 – Adult	I / G*	Visual processing speed and visual-motor skills *Written (group/individual) Oral (individual)	92	✓
Test of Word Reading Efficiency (TOWRE) USA / 1999	6 – 24:11	I	Reading efficiency for single sight words and non-words	91	✓
Wide Range Assessment of Memory and Learning - 2nd edition (WRAML-2) USA / 2003	5 - 90	I	Verbal and visual memory	90	✓
Wide Range Intelligence Test (WRIT) USA / 2000	4 – 84	I	Verbal and nonverbal ability	94	✓
Wordchains UK / 1999	7 – 18	I / G	Visual tracking skills / efficiency	91	

*Use: I denotes individual; G denotes group test administration

13. Test References

Access Reading Test, 2006, McCarty C and Crumpler M: Hodder Education

Adult Reading Test (ART), 2004, Brooks P, Everatt J and Fidler R: Roehampton University

Allcock Assessment of Handwriting Speed, 2001, Allcock P: Patoss website www.patoss-dyslexia.org

Automated Working Memory Assessment (AWMA), 2007, Packiam Alloway T: Pearson Assessment

Beery Buktenica Developmental Test of Visual-Motor Integration – 6th edition (BEERY VMI), 2010, Beery KE, Buktenica NA & Beery NA: Pearson Assessment

British Picture Vocabulary Test – 3rd edition (BPVS III), 2009, Dunn LM & Dunn DM: NFER Nelson

Comprehensive Test of Phonological Processing (CTOPP), 1999, Wagner R, Torgeson JK and Rashotte C: Pro Ed

Detailed Assessment of Speed of Handwriting (DASH), 2007, Barnett A, Henderson S, Scheib B and Schulz J: Pearson Assessment

Detailed Assessment of Speed of Handwriting (DASH 17+), 2010, Barnett A, Henderson S, Scheib B and Schulz J: Pearson Assessment

Diagnostic Reading Analysis – 2nd edition (DRA), 2004, Crumpler M & McCarty C: Hodder Education

Diagnostic Spelling Tests, 2006, Crumpler M and McCarty C: Hodder Education

Digit Memory Test, Rev. 2004, Ridsdale J & Turner M: Dyslexia Action [http://www.dyslexiaaction.org.uk/assessment-resources-for-specialist-teachers/c2f05120-6bd4-42ad-968a-eca3211ee1b3]

Dyslexia Portfolio, 2008, Turner, M: G L Assessment

Dyslexia Screening Test – Secondary (DST-S), 2004 & **Dyslexia Adult Screening Test (DAST),** 1998, Fawcett A & Nicholson R, Harcourt Assessment

Edinburgh Reading Test – 4th edition (ERT4), 2002, Educational Assessment Unit, University of Edinburgh: Hodder & Stoughton

Edinburgh Reading Test 4 – Interactive (ERT4i), 2002, Educational Assessment Unit, University of Edinburgh: Hodder & Stoughton

Expressive Vocabulary Test – 2nd edition (EVT-2), 2007, Williams K: Pearson Assessment

Gray Oral Reading Tests – 4th edition (GORT- 4), 2001, Wiederholt J L and Bryant R: Pro Ed

Gray Silent Reading Test (GSRT), 2000, Wiederholt JL and Blalock G: Pro Ed

Helen Arkell Spelling Test (HAST),1998, Brooks PL and McLean B: Helen Arkell Dyslexia Centre

Hodder Group Reading Tests – New Edition (HGRT), 2007, Vincent D and Crumpler M: Hodder Education

Hodder Oral Reading Tests (HORT), 2006, Vincent D and Crumpler M: Hodder Education

Kaufman Brief Intelligence Test – 2nd edition (K-BIT), 2004, Kaufman AS and Kaufman NL: Pearson Assessment USA

Lucid Exact, 2009, Ferrier J and Horne J: Lucid Innovations Ltd

Morrisby Manual Dexterity Test, part of Morrisby Profile 1991(revised), 2003, Morrisby J R, Morrisby MJ and Fox GD: The Morrisby Organisation

Naglieri Nonverbal Ability Test (NNAT), 2003, Naglieri JA: Pearson USA

Nonword Reading Test (NWRT), 2004, Crumpler M & McCarty C: Hodder Education

Peabody Picture Vocabulary Test - 4th edition (PPVT- 4), 2007, Dunn LM and Dunn DM: Pearson Assessment

Perin's Spoonerism Test, 1983, Perin D: Available from Dyslexia Action website [http://www.dyslexiaaction.org.uk/assessment-resources-for-specialist-teachers/c2f05120-6bd4-42ad-968a-eca3211ee1b3]

Phonological Assessment Battery (PhAB), 1997, Fredrickson N, Frith U & Reason R: NFER Nelson

Ravens Progressive Matrices & Vocabulary Scales, 2008, Raven JC, Court JH, and Raven J: Pearson Assessment

Sentence Completion Test, Hedderly R, Available from Dyslexia Action website [http://www.dyslexiaaction.org.uk/assessment-resources-for-specialist-teachers/c2f05120-6bd4-42ad-968a-eca3211ee1b3]

Single Word Reading Test (SWRT), 2007, Foster H: GL Assessment

Symbol Digit Modalities Test (SDMT), 1982, Smith A: Western Psychological Services

Test of Word Reading Efficiency (TOWRE), 1999, Torgesen JK, Wagner R and Rashotte C: Pro Ed

Vernon Graded Word Spelling Test - 3rd edition, 2006, Vernon P E: Hodder Education

Wechsler Individual Achievement Test – 2nd UK edition For Teachers (WIAT-II-UK-T), 2006, Wechsler D: Pearson Assessment

Wide Range Achievement Test – 4th edition (WRAT-4), 2006, Wilkinson GS and Robertson GJ: Psychological Assessment Resources Inc

Wide Range Achievement Test – Expanded (WRAT-E), 2001, Wilkinson G S and Robertson GJ: Psychological Assessment Resources Inc

Wide Range Assessment of Memory and Learning – 2nd edition (WRAML-2), 2003, Sheslow D and Adams W: Psychological Assessment Resources Inc

Wide Range Intelligence Test (WRIT), 2000, Glutting J, Adams W and Sheslow D: Psychological Assessment Resources Inc

Wordchains, 1999, Guron LM: NFER Nelson

Working Memory Test Battery for Children (WMTB-C), 2001, Pickering S & Gathercole S: Pearson Assessment

York Assessment of Reading for Comprehension – Passage Reading Secondary, 2010, Snowling MJ, Stothard SE, Clance P, Bowyer-Crane CD, Harrington A, Truelove E and Hulme C: GL Assessment

Some source contact websites:

- ❏ Ann Arbor www.annarbor.co.uk
- ❏ Dyslexia Action www.dyslexiaaction.org.uk
- ❏ Helen Arkell Dyslexia Centre www.arkellcentre.org.uk
- ❏ Hodder Edducation www.hoddereducation.co.uk
- ❏ Hogrefe Limited www.hogrefe.co.uk
- ❏ NFER Nelson www.nfer.ac.uk
- ❏ Patoss www.patoss-dyslexia.org
- ❏ Pearson www.psychcorp.co.uk
- ❏ The Morrisby Organisation www.morrisby.co.uk

Appendix 1: List of Acronyms

AAO	Access Arrangements Online
AB	Awarding Body
ALS	Additional Learning Support
APC	Assessment Practising Certificate
BDA	British Dyslexia Association
BPS	British Psychological Society
CPD	Continuing Professional Development
DfE	Department for Education
DfES	Department for Education and Skills
DBIS	Department for Business, Innovation and Skills
DCD	Developmental Co-ordination Disorder
DCSF	Department for Children, Schools and Families
DSA	Disabled Students Allowances
FE	Further Education
GCSE	General Certificate of Secondary Education
GCE	General Certificate of Education
HADC	Helen Arkell Dyslexia Centre
HE	Higher Education
IEP / ILP	Individual Education Plan / Individual Learning Plan
JCQ	Joint Council for Qualifications
NLS	National Literacy Strategy
OLM	Oral Language Modifier
Patoss	Professional Association of Teachers of Students with SpLD
QCDA	Qualifications and Curriculum Development Agency
SpLD	Specific Learning Difficulty
SASC	SpLD Assessment Standards Committee
SD	Standard Deviation
SEM	Standard Error of Measurement
SS	Standard Score
SEN	Special Educational Need
SENCO	Special Educational Needs Co-ordinator

Dyslexia? Assessing and Reporting, The Patoss Guide

Edited by Gill Backhouse and Kath Morris

This book focuses on the purposes, principles and practicalities of assessing for dyslexia across successive age groups, exploring the changing assessment issues and specific assessment needs.

Assessments are needed to diagnose, to plan intervention, to inform school/college policies, to support claims for funding, to justify access arrangements in examinations, and more. These very different purposes require Specialist Teachers and support managers to have a firm grasp of relevant legislation and professional guidelines, to select appropriate assessments and provide reports that will meet their intended purpose.

Dyslexia? Assessing and Reporting will enable you to achieve this! Down to earth, and with numerous examples, this book provides the practical guidance needed by Specialist Teachers and educational professionals in training, as well as by SENCOs and learning support staff working in schools and colleges.

It looks at the available types of assessments at each stage, explaining how to interpret results and how and when to involve other professionals. Throughout, special emphasis is placed upon the need to cooperate and communicate effectively with others—pupils/students, their parents, class teachers, administrators and fellow professionals—to ensure that appropriate intervention and follow-up support are forthcoming.

Edited by Gill Backhouse and Kath Morris who have both been involved as external verifiers for the OCR SpLD Training Programmes, this book also features contributions from a wealth of other specialists to cover all age ranges. It aims to share good practice throughout the assessment process.

Published by Hodder Murray in association with Patoss.

Available from Bookpoint Ltd, Hodder Murray Direct Services,
FREEPOST OF 1488, Abingdon, Oxon, OX14 4YY
Tel: 01235 827720   Fax: 01235 400454   Email: schools@bookpoint.co.uk
Paperback, 208 pp,   ISBN 978 0 340 90019 2

How Dyslexics Learn
Grasping the Nettle

by
Dr Kate Saunders and Annie White

Recognising learning strengths is a key element to successful teaching. This book concentrates on the successful strategies dyslexics have used and the positive traits associated with dyslexic learners.

"By dyslexics for dyslexics of all ages, this is the first book on the subject which one can honestly say is without fault. This book is full of practical and imaginative examples of 'How to…'. Above all, it shows the learning process for what it truly is – fun!

Susan Parkinson
Arts Dyslexia Trust

"It's readable, practical, realistic, inspirational and humbling. I will definitely be putting the ideas to use and recommending it to friends and colleagues far and wide. My only regret is I didn't read it earlier!'

Susan Cunningham
Class Teacher, Scotland

"With topics ranging from letter formation and tricky times tables to preparing for national exams, this book covers a lot without overloading its readers. It's the sort of book you need to put your name on right away because your colleagues will keep wanting to borrow it!

Maggie Powell
Hospital Teacher for Special Magazine

Chapters include:

Place in a Sunny Position – Convey the potential of the dyslexic learner

Dig a Little Deeper – Discover how dyslexics learn most effectively

Be Creative with Colour – Use imagination when teaching spelling

Cut Out the Dead Wood – Reading for a purpose

Plant Out in Neat Rows – How dyslexics learn handwriting

Deal with Garden Pests – Teach dyslexics to prepare for examinations

Gardening by Numbers – How dyslexics learn mathematics

Forcing Rhubarb – Working within the National Literacy Framework

Written to be easily understood by teachers of dyslexic learners, other professionals working in the field, non-specialist teachers, parents and adult dyslexics it avoids technical jargon. The excellent colour illustrations help bring to life the multi-memory techniques described in this refreshing resource.

Available from Patoss, www.patoss-dyslexia.org
Tel: 01386 712650   Fax: 01386 712716   email: patoss@sworcs.ac.uk
101pp, paperback   ISBN 0 9539315 1 X
Price £19.95 plus £2.75 packing and postage